Evil

Evil

Michel Wieviorka

Translated by Kristin Couper-Lobel

polity

First published in French as 'Critique du sujet', 'Penser global', 'Sortir de la violence', 'Le terrorisme global', and 'Le retour du racisme' in *Neuf leçons de sociologie* © Éditions Robert Laffont, 2008

'Facing Evil: A Sociological Perspective' © Michel Wieviorka, 2011

With kind permission from Springer Science+Business Media: Control of Violence, 2011, An End to Violence, pp. 15–40 (notes pp. 40–3), Michel Wieviorka.

Ouvrage publié avec le concours du Ministère français de la Culture-Centre national du livre.

Published with the assistance of the French Ministry of Culture-National Centre for the Book.

Polity Press
65 Bridge Street
Cambridge CB2 1UR, UK

Polity Press
350 Main Street
Malden, MA 02148, USA

ISBN-13: 978-0-7456-5392-1
ISBN-13: 978-0-7456-5393-8(pb)

A catalogue record for this book is available from the British Library.

Typeset in 11 on 13 pt Sabon
by Toppan Best-set Premedia Limited
Printed and bound in Great Britain by MPG Books Group Limited

The publisher has used its best endeavours to ensure that the URLs for external websites referred to in this book are correct and active at the time of going to press. However, the publisher has no responsibility for the websites and can make no guarantee that a site will remain live or that the content is or will remain appropriate.

Every effort has been made to trace all copyright holders, but if any have been inadvertently overlooked the publisher will be pleased to include any necessary credits in any subsequent reprint or edition.

For further information on Polity, visit our website: www.politybooks.com

Contents

Preface

When John Thompson from Polity Press suggested publishing part of my book *Neuf leçons de sociologie* (*Nine Lessons in Sociology*)[1] for an English-speaking public, my first reaction was rather mixed. For a French author, to be translated into English means reaching a truly worldwide audience, which is exceedingly gratifying; but to see one's work truncated is obviously not so pleasant – my ink is my lifeblood!

But John immediately explained his thinking: focus on keeping the chapters in my book on violence, terrorism, and racism which form a coherent whole and provide ultimately a more general perspective on the categories which enable us to integrate this whole into a broader sociological panorama. In sum, it was thus a question of abandoning the chapters devoted to themes with a positive tendency – for example, cultural difference or the commitment of the intellectual – and concentrating on those devoted to negative themes or sources of concern. I therefore uttered the word 'Evil' in English, which came to me at the time, and, in the end, I thought John's idea excellent. All that remained was to give this project its full scope, which demanded an unpublished introductory chapter, which I have written with pleasure.

This book is therefore rather different from the original version, in which there was a balance between good and evil, dealing, for example, with the construction of the individual subject as well as with its destruction, with the recognition or the respect of specificities as well as with their violent negation. This book is entirely devoted to evil, proposing an approach which is unusual in the social sciences. I am grateful to John Thompson for affording me the opportunity of reaching a new readership in what is, ultimately, a much newer and more original manner, including for myself, than an integral translation of the French version would have been.

1

Facing Evil
A Sociological Perspective

There are those who discover the subject in themselves and in others: they are the ones who do good. And there are those who seek to kill the subject in others and in themselves; they are the ones who do evil. ... And it is through a consciousness of evil that we hear, whether or not we are believers, the appeal to the subject.

Alain Touraine, *A New Paradigm for Understanding Today's World*[1]

Evil is not a category usually associated with the traditional social sciences – it is much more likely to be found in philosophy or religion. In an oft-quoted phrase, Leibniz (*Theodicy Essays*, Part One, § 21) lists three dimensions of evil more specifically: '*Metaphysical evil* consists in mere imperfection, *physical evil* in suffering, and *moral evil* in sin.'

By breaking with faith and beliefs as an explanation of social life and refuting more broadly any meta-social principle of analysis, whether it be a question of God or of Nature, the traditional social sciences eliminated evil as an explanatory principle. They could do this since evil was traditionally associated either with God – and the Devil – or else with natural, and even possibly supernatural, forces. These are entirely beyond our reach, even if they are located within us – perhaps in a magical or satanic way.

As worthy heirs of Descartes and the Enlightenment, these same traditional social sciences throughout the first major phase of the history of modernity made a distinction between body and mind and showed no interest whatsoever in suffering. Now suffering combines physical pain and the pain of the possibility of actually existing, of constructing oneself. To understand this form of suffering, body and soul or the mind must be integrated in one and the same analysis. The more the traditional social sciences endeavoured to be objective, rational, and scientific, the more determined they were to eliminate evil, which to them was a non-scientific category.

But since the 1970s a significant development has been at work, with the result that we can now speak of a post-classical age for the social sciences. At the moment, a fundamental change is taking place; the approach to their subjects is different and the subjects themselves are no longer those of the classical age. As a result, evil could become a category in the social sciences.

A major transformation

The social sciences have always been interested in God and religion; this was even perhaps their first and most critical concern. But for their representatives in the classical era, the aim was primarily to understand religious beliefs, to study them and, for some thinkers, to oppose them. At the time, modernity was more especially triumphant as traditions and religion were losing ground in favour of the universal values of reason and law; modernity was the opposite of tradition and religion. But today God has returned to societies which, until recently, were justified in believing that they were becoming totally secularized, or, to use Max Weber's words, in a process of 'disenchantment'. Beyond the inadequate and already over-worked idea of 'post-modernity' we are learning to think of present-day modernity as being two-fold: on the one hand, involving a capacity to articulate reasoning and law, both of which are undeniably fundamental components, and no longer to oppose them; and, on the other, involving convictions, choices of identity, passions, and emotions – something which has long been perceived as foreign or threatening to projects originating in the Enlightenment. Secularization can no longer be synonymous with laicization, the disappearance of faith and religion. In today's democratic societies secularization is becoming a relativization of the religious, of faith. Democracy can accommodate religion as long as it does not totally take over the lives of believers; as long as it is not a whole encroaching on all the aspects of individual or collective action and thought.

*

Since the 1970s we have fully adopted many of the dimensions of ecologist thought and we reject the idea of a total separation between nature and culture. Nature is also what we make of it, and for the vast majority of those who think about it, it is not only a question of protecting it or preserving it as it is, as in *deep ecology*. The greater our concern for the future of the planet and, at the same time our desire to protect the future of our children and of all humankind, the more we are led to integrate the 'protection' of nature and the environment in public or private policies, in innovative, constructive, concrete initiatives – this is the spirit of 'sustainable development' which has had considerable success over the past thirty years.

We approach the major environmental issues – climate, water, pollution, deforestation, or biodiversity – knowing full well that they involve humanity and not only nature. A so-called 'natural' catastrophe, for example, always includes – beforehand (before they occur), at the time (when they occur), and afterwards (when dealing with the damage) – human and social dimensions. Beforehand: depending on whether or not any provision has been made and whether or not certain measures have been taken, the extent of the tragic turn of events is more or less terrifying. For example, when a tsunami occurs, the extent of the damage caused depends on whether the choice of residential locations and of construction techniques has taken this possibility into account; the damage also depends on whether warning systems exist and are in working order, enabling the populations concerned to be alerted rapidly, and whether or not they have been informed, prepared, and possibly trained. At the time and afterwards, 'natural' catastrophes do not usually have the same impact on the rich as they have on the poor or on rulers as on the ruled. When hurricane Katrina destroyed New Orleans on 29 August 2005, it was better to be white and rich than black and poor as regards leaving the town, then, for many who had remained, as regards being rescued or helped. The effects of Katrina would have been considerably lessened if, beforehand, the levee system and the pumping of the waters of the Mississippi had been maintained and modernized by the public authorities. Thereafter the social effects of the damage were profoundly unequal. This type of observation is valid in situations of catastrophe but also for major structural problems – for climate change, for example, or issues associated with water.

Finally, our relation to the human body has considerably changed, including in the aspects perceived by present-day social sciences. In the industrial societies of yesteryear, the bodies of the ruled constituted primarily a labour force which could be exploited; weakened, damaged, and destroyed by living conditions, including illness, lack of hygiene, malnutrition, or the ravages of alcohol. Those who thought about it endeavoured to avoid this damage, to cure and to save, whence the importance of public health measures and subsequently industrial or occupational medicine. When it came to extolling the worker's body, as in the so-called 'people's democracies' in the ex-Soviet Empire, it was to showcase its muscles and productive strength, its capacity to strain every sinew towards production. More generally, at least since Descartes, it has long been customary in thinking to dissociate body and mind, and the traditional social sciences were not particularly interested in the body as such. But today, numerous individuals work *on* their bodies and not only *with* their bodies. They do classes in music and movement, dance, sport, yoga, and these activities now occupy a considerable part of their lives, including among the working class. The body is also the object of care as well as markings in ways which are not so much imposed by the culture and society as decided upon individually, as a set of individual choices. The skin (make-up, but also tattooing) and hair especially give rise to huge markets which the cosmetic industries in particular exploit.

Over the past thirty years, consideration of the links between body and mind has been furthered by progress in the neurosciences and the cognitive sciences and by the idea that it is possible if not to fill, at least to reduce the gap between psychology and biology and to try to match the analyses which come under each of these headings.

*

Finally, evil is linked with suffering, which can be both physical and mental. There again, recent events call for the development of research on pain and no longer for explanations using the concept of evil. Under the impact of patients' movements, the mobilization of nursing staff and public opinion campaigns, our societies are now much more aware of pain. This is particularly clear if we consider health care systems. In many countries, specialized services are developing offering palliative care: that is, dealing with the suffering of patients whom we do not know, or no longer know, how to treat. Equally, there are discussions about euthanasia, and the possibility of deciding to put an end to human existence for individuals faced with a certain death as well as considerable suffering and who themselves, if they are conscious, wish to die. Recent trends are towards the medicalization of euthanasia, making it a medical decision, and towards the de-medicalization of palliative care. Thus our societies are learning how to care for patients and not simply disease, and to think about the dying and not only of death.

Pain here is treated as a problem which is both individual – each time there is suffering – and collective – since it involves institutional care. It is not treated as an external natural or divine curse. As everything concerning illness and death clearly reveals, the sociology of evil is advancing – all the more so since our societies perceive themselves as being composed of individual subjects, all of whom are to some extent fragile or vulnerable, each with his or her own subjectivity, which is itself constantly subjected to processes of subjectivization or de-subjectivization.

Thus, former differences are becoming blurred. The place of God and that of nature are changing. The separation between body and soul is challenged. Hence, to return to the categories of Leibniz, whether it be metaphysical, physical or moral, in all cases, the change in collective life and in the paradigms of the social sciences as well as their objects of study is opening up a larger space for the sociological study of evil and pain.

Ethics and human rights

This space where evil and pain become objects for the social sciences and no longer explanatory principles or non-social or non-human phenomena is further enlarged if we take into consideration the major transformations in the spheres of ethics and human rights.

Traditionally, ethics proposes philosophical rules of conduct, possibly transcribed into norms and in laws which direct concrete decision-making. Ethics overarches collective life; prior to any action, it lays down concepts of good and evil, just and unjust, right and wrong. It structures choices by proposing general principles which then only remain to be applied, even if these can, and perhaps must, be interpreted and therefore actors do have a degree of latitude.

But there is a tangible change taking place in democracies towards what one might call bottom-up ethics: in this case the decision is prepared, if not taken, as closely as possible to the situation. In these circumstances, ethics is not, or is not uniquely, an abstract corpus of rules and principles, but the outcome of a demanding discussion between the people concerned, but not necessarily involved. Thus, clinical medical ethics, in the hospitals which have chosen to make it systematic and to institutionalize it, is based on the existence of an ethics consultation service in which medical personnel (doctors, nurses), lawyers, philosophers and social science researchers, and so on, meet with one another. Whenever a difficult question of life or death occurs in the hospital, this service can be consulted. It carries out an inquiry, meets the people concerned, confronts points of view and sheds light on a decision which does not come within its remit but which is made in close consultation with it. Bottom-up ethics is not necessarily in contradiction with more traditional forms of ethics; some people consider it to be simply a form of 'applied ethics', to use an expression which appeared in the United States in the 1960s. The spheres of this 'application' are numerous – the philosopher Paul Ricoeur in the 1990s was already referring to bioethics, environmental ethics, business and professional ethics, and noted that they were 'taught and practised in universities, companies, hospitals [as we saw], at governmental and international levels'.[2] The 'good' – in other words the preparation for a decision which is the best (or the least bad) possible – is the outcome of a collective approach on the ground, case by case. It is not fixed in advance. Good – and therefore also evil, its opposite – will become part of the intellectual sphere of these disciplines as the participation of social science researchers in this preparation increases.

History is in society

There are also profound changes in history; the most critical of these are closely related to the incursion of memories into the public sphere. Since the 1960s we have witnessed what Anthony Smith,[3] one of the first to have perceived the extent of the phenomenon, called an 'ethnic revival' – an expression which does not adequately account for the spectacular development of the phenomenon since the 1980s. Throughout the world, voices have been making themselves heard, focusing not so much – or not only – on an ethnic type of identity – that is, one which links cultural dimensions and references to nature, and even race – but also on a status of historical – and possibly present-day – victim. Actors are demanding recognition in the name of a community, of a past involving extreme violence: genocide, ethnocide, mass killings, slave trade, brutal colonization, and so on. In numerous cases demands for recognition of historical suffering are associated with demands linked to racism or discrimination suffered here and now by the members of these same groups. For example, being an African-American in the United States means highlighting a culture, a literature, musical forms, and so on; it also means recalling the slave trade, slavery, then the racism experienced in the past. Finally, it also involves denouncing the structural racism still at work in American society today. This upsurge is so important that it gives rise to a highly competitive situation where groups jostle one another in the public eye to display their past and the injustices suffered yesterday and today. A Belgian sociologist, Jean-Michel Chaumont,[4] has called this 'victims in competition'.

One consequence of the thriving demands for the recognition of identities, possibly of victimization, is that they upset the history of the country in question and challenge the nation which this history presents. History, and in particular the history in school textbooks and in education, is destabilized by the incursion of these memories, which it resists and on the basis of which it can also be transformed. What is at stake is an inversion, or in any case a considerable modification, of the classical paradigm which makes of history a national narrative. Yesterday, societies and nations were located in history and many philosophies aspired to an explanation of its meaning. Today it is the opposite: history, via memory, is located in society, foraging into it and modifying it with the incursion of demands for remembrance which transform the nation, forcing it to change its historical narrative. History as a narrative has become a force of change.

Yesterday, the socialization of children, or migrants, involved learning the national historical narrative; today, migrants and their children contribute to changing this narrative, forcing the nation to recognize the less glorious pages of its past, its areas of darkness and practices of violence and brutality. From this point on, evil becomes an object for the social sciences: they have to give a convincing account, on one hand, of the past and the present of the groups who mobilize on the basis of an identity or as victims; and, on the other, of the impact of their demands on community life. How was violence organized in the past, or how is it organized in the present; and how do the processes of negation of the Other, of destruction and self-destruction, of harm to one's physical and moral integrity, function?

It is no longer possible to declare, as it was until recently, that to try to understand barbarism, violence, cruelty, terrorism or racism is to open the way to evil, which needs quite simply to be fought without making any effort to understand – any effort of that kind being automatically classed as a mark of weakness. In fact, if we do wish to combat evil, it is preferable to know and understand it. There is a need here, a social demand which calls for analytical tools and studies; the social sciences are better qualified to provide these than moral judgements, philosophical considerations or religious a priori.

Democracy, justice, and forgiveness

The way in which human rights have developed since the end of the Second World War also contributes to enlarging the arena for new approaches to evil. Nowadays, human rights are the concern not only of religious or political forces, intellectuals or a few associations, or some states or international organizations like the United Nations or UNESCO, but also, on an increasingly large scale, of NGOs. These are evidence of the existence of national civil societies which fall within the framework of a nation-state, but perhaps also even, according to some analyses, of a nascent civil society at world level; in any event their conscience is global. Their action frequently aims at thwarting or confronting the consequences of one or other form of turmoil: war and its damages, the consequences of 'natural' disasters, mortality, hunger, forced migration, and so on. For them, the issue at stake, without the shadow of a doubt, is not to confront only or mainly purely natural forces, and, even less, divine ones, but the consequences of the devastating effects of human actions.

Other perspectives have opened up, once again recently, with the rise in apologies and requests for forgiveness emanating from heads of state or those in charge of important institutions. In the past, there was no question of recognizing wrongs, but now Queen Elizabeth II has apologized for the racial violence imposed by the British on the Maoris of New Zealand; the Catholic Church has recanted on its assimilationist policy, which to a large extent contributed to the destruction of the Aborigines in Australia, or has apologized for the paedophilia of a number of its priests; the Lutheran Church in America has apologized for the anti-Semitism of Martin Luther, and so on. South Africa after apartheid inaugurated an original practice of institutional and legal forgiveness with the Truth and Reconciliation Commission, which inspired numerous other experiences, in particular in Latin America. This type of practice, whereby the processing of the effects of evil is dealt with by democratic bodies in which the actors express themselves, explain themselves, reply, can ask forgiveness, and so on, constitutes a further encouragement to make of turmoil a social, political, legal, or cultural problem rather than something absolute, and avoids it becoming a purely moral, religious, or metaphysical category. And it is not because evil is now associated with the implication of the actors and the idea of a conscience and a responsibility that action to confront it can be reduced to repression and punishment. Democracy, by becoming more participative and deliberative, like justice, in particular when the intention is to make reparation, both involve, on the contrary, collective thinking about specific expressions of evil, on the basis of which other approaches than that of punishment can be used. This is what happens, for example, when someone who is guilty of a crime, instead of being sentenced to prison, is asked to make amends to the victim in some way or to accept a period of community service. Evil becomes a sociological category and ceases to be a purely religious category when it is treated as a crime, including a crime against humanity, and not as a sin; when it can and must be envisaged as a social and historical problem that falls within the scope of human will and justice, and when it ceases to be a theological fact or the manifestation of an instinct.

The unity of evil

When speaking about evil, we postulate a unity of some sort, so much so that in some languages or certain written texts a capital letter is used – Evil. This unity may lead to a definition which would attempt to suggest there is a common denominator to what tends to be a set of rather different experiences – in this publication, for example, we will deal more specifically with violence, terrorism, and racism. In all cases, from the social science point of view, evil is the outcome of human action and implies degradation, destruction, negation, in any event a challenge to the physical, mental, or moral integrity of certain people or groups, directly or indirectly.

But it is best to avoid reifying or deifying evil, postulating a unity which would make it an absolute and therefore would always risk making it a principle exterior to humankind. There may be a general inherence of evil, consubstantial with human nature, a probability which spares nobody, with the result that in certain circumstances cruelty, gratuitous violence, and sadism arise. In other words, it is possible that there is a hard core of evil which is unavoidable.

The present-day vocation of the social sciences in this instance is not to make a sociology of everything, but to get as close as we can to this hard core; to reduce it as much as we are able to and to reveal as far as possible the social, anthropological, historical, psychological dimensions of the various forms which evil may take. And if a hard core of this type subsists, resisting this type of approach, a set of dimensions of evil which research of the sociological, or social anthropological, type cannot shed light on, then perhaps we can suggest a concept of 'pure' evil for this.

There is something paradoxical about a concept of this type. 'Pure Evil' – and perhaps this is an instance which requires the capital letter – would be what remains of the various expressions of 'evil' in general, after eliminating all the aspects which can be included in the explanations offered by the social sciences. Therefore 'pure Evil' would be something residual, at the same time as being the extreme, highly refined, form of what in material, historical reality appears in 'unrefined forms' – that is to say, to a large extent covered by these explanations.

If evil lies within society and has not come from without by some sort of evil spell, whether natural or divine, if it is human, if it is a consequence of our action, then we have to ask the leading questions concerning the guilt, the conscience and the responsibility of its perpetrators, as well as of those who endeavour to combat it. The idea of total non-responsibility which would make of the perpetrator of evil a non-actor, the performer of an instruction or an order emanating from an authority considered legitimate without having to ask the slightest question, becomes unacceptable except in extreme and very special cases. If, as in the phrase coined by Hannah Arendt, evil can be manifested in the form of 'banality', this does not automatically mean not being responsible or lack of conscience. In *Eichmann in Jerusalem*,[5] Arendt described the Nazi criminal from the point of view of the 'banality of evil', by observing that his defence was to plead he was not responsible: according to Eichmann, the crimes committed were carried out wholly in response to an order, in the name of a legitimate higher authority, with no personal emotion involved – if he had been ordered to kill his own father, he would have done it, he said. But was there really no commitment on his part to the Nazi project, absolutely no trace of anti-Semitism in Eichmann? Nobody can seriously believe this.

The closer evil comes to corresponding to the categories and concerns of the social sciences, the more their analytical principles must be applied, in the same way as they are used to study other problems or other social facts. Amongst these principles there is the idea that actors are never either totally unaware or totally aware of the meaning of their action. In other words they are never totally non-responsible; they are of necessity accountable for their actions, or they should be. In this sense, the advance of the knowledge of evil, thanks to the social sciences, goes hand in hand with the idea that the thesis of the banality of evil must be, if not set to one side, at least considered with the utmost caution.

*

Thus, in opening up to evil, the social sciences are not finding a new vocation for themselves or renewing an interest in metaphysics, physics, or moral philosophy. They are not appropriating registers which were not theirs, because, on the contrary, to a large extent they constructed themselves precisely by freeing themselves from these registers, possibly even opposing them. They put a name to the issues or the problems which they accept to confront; they implement research which is based on methods and paradigms specific to them, by asserting that evil, like good, is human – neither is external to human beings or to the relations which they maintain with one another. Good and evil are not acts of God or of nature but are part of the everyday reality of collective life.

This book therefore sets out an approach to evil which frees it from its infra- or meta-social connotations, making it an object for analysis, undoubtedly singular and with its own specificities, but not to the point of being considered radically different from any other object. Rather than risking making 'evil' an absolute, this book considers relatively specific, concrete, important forms: violence, terrorism, and racism.

These are questions to which I have devoted much lengthy research. For all that, this book does not offer original, empirical knowledge. It is intended as a contribution to introduce in a somewhat systematic way a concrete sociology of evil that is given credibility by being based on tangible experience.

2

An End to Violence

The Subject and violence

There can be no discussion of violence today without involving the notions of Subject or subjectivity, in various ways.

Objectivity and subjectivity

The first thing that has to be stated is that the threat remains of the disarticulation between objective approaches to violence, which may be quantified and which can claim to be universal as they are theoretically acceptable to all, and subjective or relative approaches, which look at what an individual, a group, or a society considers as such at any given time. A legal definition of violence, centred on the state and, in the words of Max Weber, on a legitimate monopoly of force, appears to enable this problem to be set aside and violence simply to be objectivized. In this context, André Lalande's *Vocabulaire technique et critique de la philosophie*, backed up by Montesquieu, mentions the 'illegitimate or at least illegal use of force'.[1] But when the state entrusts private agents with a substantial part of war-making, as is overwhelmingly evident with the US intervention in Iraq,[2] and when internal security is likewise handed over to the private sector, a trend currently at work worldwide, the state monopoly of legitimate force is called into question, as is the possibility of discussing violence objectively, as in Lalande's definition quoted above.

The advent of the age of victims that began in the 1960s considerably strengthens this process of calling into question, and the upsurge of individual identities has considerable 'memory' and 'victim' dimensions. Many actors nowadays are demanding acknowledgement of and, in some cases, reparation for the crimes perpetrated upon their forebears and, at the same time, appearing in the public arena in connection with the harsh injustices they have suffered or, indeed, may still be suffering to this day. Such movements can be cultural, religious, or ethnic, perhaps national, black, or Indian; they may involve the survivors of genocide or their descendants, or the parents or children of victims of a dictatorship or totalitarian power. Such actors portray past and present violence not so much from the point of view of the threat to order or calling the state into question, but rather as an experience undergone and its consequences on those undergoing it; they speak of the trauma suffered and its effects over time, for example. Here, violence equals negation of or an attack on an individual's physical and moral integrity, with implications that may affect succeeding generations. This makes it difficult to develop as a Subject; it invades subjectivity and takes the place of a subjectivization process. From this viewpoint, violence affects individual, personal and collective existences.

The tension between the objectivity and subjectivity of violence is not a purely theoretical problem; it can lead to fierce political debate. In France during the 1980s and 1990s, for example, people wondered whether delinquency and crime were increasing objectively, or whether it was in fact the feeling of insecurity that had increased, without any automatic link with an actual increase in crime, as the left claimed (before gradually moving away from this view of the problem). The harder it is to establish a direct link between acts of violence and their representations, the more the understanding of the one and the other falls into two separate registers which ultimately are almost completely dissociated.

Classical approaches

When thinking about an end to violence, it is not sufficient just to consider the victims and their subjectivity, however important their point of view may be and however consider-able may be their ability to mobilize opinion and the media and to appeal to the state and political leaders. One must also look at the actors involved in violence. Yet conventional methods of analysis are scarcely ever concerned with their subjectivity.

Some people see violence as crisis behaviour, a response to changes in their situation causing one or more players to react, often out of frustration. This approach gains respect-ability with Alexis de Tocqueville, who explains à propos of the French Revolution that violence was especially marked when the population found its situation improving: 'One would say', he wrote, 'that the French found their situation the more unbearable as it improved.'[3] Above all, though, it was British and American functionalist or neo-functionalist researchers who were responsible for the rise of this thesis, in the form of the theory of relative frustration, in the 1960s and 1970s. The idea put forward by James Davies, for example, and taken up to a considerable degree by Ted Robert Gurr,[4] is in fact that violence develops when the gap between a group's expectations and the scope for fulfilling them widens to the point of being intolerable. This type of approach has sometimes produced interesting results. However, in the 1970s various studies revealed its shortcom-ings and very limited explanatory power.

Very differently, a second type of analysis stresses the rational, instrumental nature of violence, including in its collective dimensions – riots and revolution, for example.

This may be said to have gained respectability with Thomas Hobbes but really took off in the 1960s, notably through the work of historian Charles Tilly. For supporters of the thesis of 'mobilization of resources', violence is a resource, a means, which is mobilized by players in order to achieve their ends. Most of the time this idea serves to explain how players excluded from the political field use violence as a way of gaining admission and staying there. Such an idea has the advantage of no longer reducing violence to the notion of reactive crisis behaviour; instead, it makes the perpetrator of violence someone who is aware of the issues surrounding the act of violence, which, in turn, consequently makes sense. This approach argues that violence should not be separated from the wider conflict in the context of which it may arise, such as industrial action or a farmers' demonstration. It has considerable explanatory power.

Finally, a third type of approach, in fact very wide and diversified, postulates a link between culture and violence. Some writers regard the progress of culture, or rather of civilization, as the opposite of violence, in the tradition of the well-known study by Norbert Elias of the process of civilization, which explains how the modern individual has learned, from etiquette at the King's Court, for example, to control his aggression and check his violent impulses.[5] Other writers stress how some cultures favour violence more than others, possibly through socialization and education – with reference, for example, to the work of Theodor Adorno on anti-Semitism.[6] One problem associated with this set of perspectives is that the analysis generally omits political and social mediation and also disregards the historical layer that may separate the time when a personality is shaped and the moment of acting.

Conventional approaches to violence should not be forgotten or rejected; they provide a perspective which may be useful in order to understand a concrete experience of violence. However, they fail to deal with certain dimensions that are nevertheless essential and which the concept of Subject offers a way of comprehending.

The Subject of violence

Violence may present aspects suggesting a process of loss of meaning: when the actor comes to express a meaning that has become lost or impossible and resorts to violence because he is unable to construct the confrontational action that would enable him to assert his social demands or cultural or political expectations, because no political process is available for dealing with them.

A lack or loss of meaning does not necessarily lead to a vacuum, a complete lack of meaning, and, ultimately, nihilism; such deficiencies often give rise to processes of manufacturing a new meaning of a more or less artificial nature – in other words, detached from reality, resulting in excesses and immoderation. In some experiences, for example, violence is based on an ideology from which it originates and which gives it a substitute meaning, as will be seen below with reference to Italian far-left terrorism. Other cases involve a myth, a discursive construction suggesting the possible integration of elements of meaning which, in fact, become increasingly contradictory. Here, violence develops when the myth disintegrates and ceases to be viable, while the actor nevertheless endeavours to keep it alive. In the modern world, though, religion often lends a meta-political meaning to a violent act which then transcends politics, even if it soon becomes established again at that level.

Violence has other aspects which continue to elude conventional approaches. This is the case when cruelty, gratuitous violence, and violence for violence's sake are involved; when the actor not only destroys another but destroys himself, wipes out his existence by murderous, martyr-style acts. Or when the perpetrator appears to attach no personal meaning to his act, presenting himself as not responsible and claiming simply to have obeyed a lawful authority. This, as noted in the previous chapter, was the line of defence put forward by Eichmann in Jerusalem, as described by Hannah Arendt.[7]

The concept of Subject may prove particularly useful for taking account of these different aspects, provided that the definition adopted is not too unimaginative or rudimentary. I, therefore, propose to establish five cases, each corresponding to a type of subjectivity that can be linked to violence.[8]

- The *Floating Subject* is one who, not managing to become an actor, resorts to violence: for instance, the young immigrant from a run-down French neighbourhood setting fire to cars during the October/November 2005 riots as his only way of expressing, if not specific social demands, then at least his desire to build a life for himself.
- The *Hyper-Subject* compensates for the loss of meaning by excess, to which he gives a new, ideological, mythical, or religious meaning. Violence here is inseparable from conviction – it is a commitment imbued with a meaning that extends well beyond the situation in which it is expressed, aiming much further. Islamic martyrism can serve as an illustration of this: the actor kills, and in so doing extinguishes his own life, combining deep despair with a meta-political vision that transports him beyond life itself.
- The *Non-Subject* acts violently without in any way involving his subjectivity, at least apparently merely obeying orders, as in Stanley Milgram's famous experiments.[9] His violence has no meaning from his point of view; it is nothing more than a form of submission to a lawful authority.
- The *Anti-Subject* is that side of the Subject that fails to acknowledge the other person's right to be a Subject and which can develop only by negating the other person's humanity. This case corresponds to the dimensions of cruelty or enjoyment of violence for its own sake, as an end in itself. Here, the victim is dehumanized, reified, or animalized and is in every respect the opposite of the Subject. The perpetrator of cruel acts who finds pleasure in violence assumes that position and acts contrary to the humanist dimensions on which the concept of subject is ordinarily based – hence the use of the term *Anti-*

Subject. Masochism is a perverted form of this scenario, in which the victim also derives pleasure from his own dehumanization.

• The *Survivor Subject* corresponds to a situation where, before any aggression has actually taken place, an individual may (rightly or wrongly – it matters not) feel that his very existence is threatened, and act violently to ensure his own survival.

This typology, briefly outlined here, certainly deserves to be developed and the proposed terminology is not perhaps the most suitable, but it should be pointed out that until now we have lacked any sociological categories to merit a fuller description of these different cases. It has the advantage of helping us to tackle the most mysterious aspect of violence, which is also the core one: not the frustrations it may reveal, nor the more or less rational calculations made by the person resorting to violence, nor even the culture from which it stems, but the processes of loss of meaning and excess of meaning through which violence may develop, the share of surplus and lack involved, the twisted, corrupted, or sometimes also perverted subjectivity that makes violence possible.

Violence and globalization

We can no longer approach the issue of violence today as we would have done only twenty or thirty years ago. The world has changed, considerably, and the processes of globalization are at the heart of these changes. By thinking 'globally', we can approach violence with a fresh or altered perspective.

The end of the Cold War

Let us look at the world as it was in the 1950s or 1960s. Essentially, it was structured by the central conflict between the two superpowers of the day: the United States, on the one hand, and the Soviet Union, on the other. The Yalta

Agreement, signed before the Second World War was even over, carved the world up into two zones of influence. The Cold War was, thus, a major ideological, economic, and geopolitical confrontation, but it never led either to head-on war or to significant unmediated local conflicts. Neither the Korean War nor the Vietnam War pitted the two superpowers directly against each other, nor did they escalate into a much wider world war; they remained localized. Nuclear weapons ensured a degree of prudence between the two blocs and had a deterrent effect; the prospect of their use restrained extremes of action, even in times of high tension, notably the Cuban Missile Crisis in 1962. Warlike violence was, thus, limited throughout the world, as many countries were more or less firmly within the sphere of influence of one or other superpower and everyone knew that a localized war was likely to lead to global conflict.

A report by the Human Security Centre[10] in Vancouver, published in October 2006, admittedly forces us to qualify the idea of a world where military violence was lessened by the Cold War. Backed up by figures, this report states that many wars were fought by proxy in the Third World in those days and there was also local violence, in some cases very bloody. One should not, therefore, paint too idyllic a picture of that period. But the Cold War did prevent the escalation, spread, or extension of war, at least in its conventional form. It also had the effect of curbing international terrorism, which was carried on mainly by actors claiming to support the Palestinian cause, who, as will be seen, never went as far as they do nowadays.

The end of the Cold War deprived the world of a way of structuring conflict which avoided military violence far more than it authorized or facilitated it. After that, new splits appeared, civil wars took on quite a different aspect, and mass outbreaks of new or renewed violence began to occur. Organized crime prospered along with globalization.

Whereas the number of conventional armed conflicts between states has decreased by 40 per cent since 1992, according to the Human Security Centre report, and the bloodiest conflicts (those that cause more than 1,000 battlefield deaths per year) have declined in number by 80 per cent; and coups d'état or attempted coups declined to 10 in 2004 compared to 25 in 1963, other forms of violence have increased. 'Global terrorism' has struck a number of times, frequently killing and injuring dozens of victims in a single attack. Generally speaking, the percentage of civilian victims compared with military victims has increased considerably. Barbarity has become established in all sorts of parts of the world, including in Europe, where one might think that after Nazism there would be no more mass crimes of a genocidal nature: the break-up of the former Yugoslavia involved violent 'ethnic cleansing', whereas in the Cold War era that country was in fact considered a factor in international stability. In Africa, moreover, the Great Lakes' genocide left more than one million people dead.

Armed conflicts now take new forms: asymmetrical wars, for example, or crisis management in a supranational or multilateral context. Military interventions, sometimes by UN-appointed multinational forces, are increasing with the aim, in theory, not of winning in order to impose power, but, rather, of bringing situations of extreme localized violence to an end. The break-up of the former Yugoslavia with violence that lasted almost throughout the 1990s, the horrors of Africa's Great Lakes with the 1994 genocide, the violence perpetrated by pro-Indonesian militias following the creation of the independent state of Timor (1999 referendum), the disastrous experience of Somalia (1992–3), the recent war in Lebanon (summer 2006), and the Darfur crisis are all new configurations of war, in which local confrontations and violence, in some cases charged with nationalist, religious, or ethnic significance, end in joint intervention by armies endeavouring, from outside the theatre of operations, to bring peace and re-energize civilian processes of restoring calm and development. Throughout the Cold War, moreover, nuclear weapons acted as a restraint and even promoted peace. Nuclear weapons have since become, or at least come to symbolize, a major risk factor, associated with images of destabilization or regional crisis, notably in the Middle East and Asia, and with considerable problems of proliferation.

Of course, the end of the Cold War does not explain everything, and a more detailed analysis ought, in geopolitical terms, also to cover, notably, the end of colonialism, the decolonization processes, and the ending of dependence for many Latin American societies. But the fall of the Berlin Wall was a turning point. At the time, the Cold War carried the stamp of violence, notably in what were termed the 'proxy' wars; its end also meant an ending of these instances of violence. Often it had prevented the intervention of the United Nations (and also of other actors, notably NGOs) in a preventive or peacekeeping role. The dawn of a new era brought with it fresh mediations, negotiations, and intervention and, thus, initiated a learning process in negotiated, democratic conflict management. On the other hand, the Cold War kept organized crime at a certain level and held international terrorism in check, because the main actors in such violence needed the 'sponsorship' of states often themselves within the sphere of influence of the Soviet Union; following its demise, the door was opened to a growth in organized crimes and more intense forms of terrorism.

The end of the Cold War did not in itself give rise to a fresh period of acts of violence (some of the most spectacular instances of which have been mentioned above), but it did play a large part in some major changes. In the words of historian Charles Tilly it meant the invention of a new repertoire of violence.[11]

The end of the industrial age

Globalization has also meant big changes in the nature of capitalism and its associated forms of domination. The old industrial age, when economic power corresponded more or less directly to social relations located primarily in the factory or workshop, has given way to a phase when production problems seem to be dissociated from problems of economic power. No longer do the bosses hold the central role of dominant players, nor, as was once thought, do the managers; nowadays that role falls to 'global' financial capitalism. Companies' profits are, therefore, measured by a different yardstick to production, and it is not uncommon for a big group's share price to rise even as it is announcing mass layoffs and the closure of factories that are still profitable – only not profitable enough for the shareholders. For modern capitalism, the short term prevails over the long term. As Richard Sennett points out, for example, 'In 1960, a company was assessed in terms of predicted profits in three years' time, whereas in 2000 that timescale has been shortened to three months on average.'[12]

All the same, conventional forms of work organization have not disappeared. Take the example of the *maquiladora* factories in Mexico, not far from the US border, most of which are dependent on big multinational groups and are part of the global economy. The forms of worker exploitation that still prevail there often seem to date from another age, so harsh are they and so impenetrable by union action or the most basic protection offered by employment law.[13] But there, as everywhere else in the world, globalization means the decline of the workers' ability to take action, a loss of impact and, even more so, of centrality for the labour movement. Economic power and, thus, the opponent, or 'other side' in the conflict for a would-be labour movement actor, is now too far removed from the site of production to allow the existence of a relationship comparable to the one that used to pit the working masses and the employers against one another while at the same time binding them, in the days when Taylorism was at its height. Capital can move at lightning speed, and the identifications that formerly inspired workers to want to become their own bosses and, thus, formed the foundation of counter-offensive protest have waned: how can anyone identify with a job, a type of work, a company, if there is no job security, if they know they will have to change their line of work several times in the course of their life, and if the company regards them as eminently 'expendable'? How is it possible to devise any long-term action involving a high degree of planning and structure if the work organization is constantly moving around and relocating and if the prevailing individualism and flexibility are depicted as the triumphant opposite of the traditional concept of worker solidarity?

The end of the old industrial age did not make the world of work more violent; rather, it led to a loss of fighting spirit, an inability to carry on mass struggles and to link them with counter-projects for society or visions of utopia. Nevertheless, it altered the arena of violence. On the one hand, during the 1970s and 1980s, violence took the form of far-left terrorism in several countries just emerging from that old order, notably Italy: students, intellectuals, and also, in some cases, workers became more radical in order to carry on, by means of armed conflict, a fight which no longer had any meaning or reality in the factories. On the other hand, the decline of the core principle of conflict provided by the labour movement left a vacuum which no other actor of similar stature stepped forward to fill, either socially or politically. Throughout the world, communism did not collapse solely because of the break-up of the Soviet Union, or the exhaustion of its ideology; its disappearance also owes a lot to the decline of the labour movement which it represented, of which it was sometimes the main representative. And if the social democratic model seems to be on its last legs, or irrelevant, in the old industrial societies, the reason is partly that it has to postulate strong ties between the party and the trade unions, in historical contexts where the unions have lost most of their power.

Now the lack of a framework for confrontation between the two sides is always a factor in a decline in social or moral standards and violence. When people's expectations are not channelled into debate and conflicts between actors, they degenerate into cynicism or fatalism, on the one hand, and crisis behaviour and violence, on the other hand. One of the reasons for the urban riots in France in October and November 2005 was the lack of any forum, in the poorer districts, for putting the demands of young people – mostly from an immigrant background – into a confrontational setting and dealing with them at a political level. Thirty or forty years previously, those same districts were 'red suburbs' where the Communist Party, as well as an active, living fabric of associations, effectively channelled social conflict with feedback at a political level. Nowadays, the Communist Party has abandoned the field and the old fabric of associations has vanished. The violent rioting, with several hundred vehicles set on fire every night for nearly three weeks, was the expression of a keen sense of dereliction and abandonment and also anger, and there was no institutionalized framework for conflict there to give it media coverage.

Apart from the experience of the end of industrial society and the decline of the labour movement, the foregoing remarks lead us to a general hypothesis that can serve as a basis for the analysis: the arena for violence is widening, while the scope for organizing debate and a framework for conflict to deal with social problems is shrinking, lacking, or vanishing. Conversely that arena becomes smaller when the conditions of institutionalized conflict permit a negotiated solution, even in circumstances of great tension between actors. Violence is not conflict; rather it is the opposite. Violence is more likely to flare up when an actor can find no-one to deal within his or her attempts to exert social or political pressure, when no channels of institutional negotiation are available.

This proposition should be considered as an analytical tool, not as a hard-and-fast rule – there are situations, experiences, or circumstances where conflict and violence go hand-in-hand. We have linked it to globalization because the more the latter is uncontrolled, purely neoliberal, and knows no borders, the more it undermines the institutions and representative bodies set up to deal with social demands within a framework of conflict. So why not wait for first attempts at establishing courts of law and supranational means of regulating economic life, or perhaps the advent of the alter-globalization movement, in the hope that they will, in time, help to redefine the image of globalization and its consequences?

An end to violence: the victims' perspective

The analytical bases described above correspond only to certain forms of violence and certain problems and, moreover, in no way permit an approach that could claim to be exhaustive. Our aim here, as throughout this contribution, is more to introduce a type of sociological approach rather than to supply systematic, heavily documented information about a particular topic. Not only does this approach indicate how one may tackle so important an issue as violence, or at least some aspects of it; but also it can extend the analysis of violence by looking at the conditions that may enable us to deal with it. Let us, therefore, return to the first of the points just made: the growing importance of the victims' point of view.

Three registers

Democracies are increasingly sensitive to the victims' viewpoint, and the themes of suffering, trauma, forgiveness, and reconciliation hold a considerable place in the public arena of democratic debate. What does an end to violence mean in a democracy when one is a victim, a descendant of victims, or a survivor? For such individuals and groups, the weighty experiences of mass killings, genocides, slavery, the slave trade, and other crimes against humanity obviously did not come to a sudden halt on the day when barbarity was ended; they left their marks. An end to violence in fact means dealing with the present-day repercussions of past sufferings.

That which is destroyed or altered, in that family of experiences, is not one-dimensional; it in fact refers, according to eminently variable conditions, to three separate registers. The first of these is collective identity. Mass destructions liquidate not only human beings, but also, to a greater or lesser degree, a culture, a way of life, a language, a religion – hence the use sometimes of the neologism 'ethnocide'. The destruction of Europe's Jews by the Nazis and their accomplices, for example, eradicated the Yiddish culture from

Central Europe and almost wiped out the language. Admittedly the language still exists, spoken for instance by the Lubavitch movement, but it no longer has the same link to living communities, as in the days of the *shtetl*, the Jewish settlement in Central and Eastern Europe. It is true, as the work of the historian Jacob Katz showed, that such communities had already been eroded by the modern world and abandoned by many of the people who lived in them even before the Second World War. But Nazism acted with unprecedented force, practically annihilating that identity, with the result that it would never again contribute anything new, vital, or dynamic to humanity. All that remains is something that has been repressed, with only survivors left to try to keep traces of it alive, at the risk of lapsing into a 'lachrymal' past, as it has been termed by the Jewish historian Salo Baron. That identity fills museums and memories, it has its own memory, but that which gave it meaning has been lost, it no longer corresponds to a constantly evolving history. Here, reparation is impossible; that which has been destroyed cannot be brought back, and irremediably belongs to the past alone.

The second register concerns individual participation in modern life. Crimes against humanity do not only affect groups external to modernity; on the contrary, those affected may be directly involved in modernity, or at least in contact with it and likely to be to some extent a party. What is concerned, therefore, is also a person's ability to exist as an individual and to have access to money, consumer goods, work, housing, health, and so on. Being a victim or the descendant of a victim, thus, means not only having been attacked in one's cultural being and physical integrity; it also means having been treated as a slave whereas, within the same society, other people were free; it means having been deprived of one's property, one's rights, the sense of belonging at civil or national level to a larger collective entity than one's group alone. To carry on the example of Nazism: the German Jews were highly integrated within German society and the German nation, almost assimilated, and when the

Nazis told them they had been rejected by society and the nation, many of them failed to understand what they were being told. The great historian and sociologist Norbert Elias, who fled to the UK in 1935, relates in an autobiographical work how his parents refused to listen when he advised them to flee Germany: nothing can happen to us, we've done nothing wrong, was the gist of what they said to him.[14] When individual participation in modernity is denied in this way by extreme violence, what is at stake is not only a collective identity, membership of a group, but an identification, more or less assumed, with universal values to which one has been a party, or which have been held up as something for everyone to aspire to, and from which one has been shut out and forcefully expelled.

Lastly there is a third register, which has to do with personal subjectivity, that ability of any human being to be a Subject. Extreme violence annihilates or at any rate severely affects the Subject. It dehumanizes the person, treating him or her like a thing or an animal, or it may demonize him or her, attributing evil powers to that individual – in the way that women, in the past, were often called witches. This is why the survivors of a barbarous tragedy sometimes feel they cannot go on living. They have ceased to believe in the humanity of the personal Subject. They have experienced its negation within themselves and they have seen it vanish from their persecutors. How can anyone live after Auschwitz, it has often been asked?

Dealing with threefold destruction

If we consider the three registers just described, putting an end to extreme violence means being able to deal with the threefold destruction that has affected, first of all, a collective identity; second, individuals inasmuch as they participate in modernity; and, third, Subjects whose humanity is denied.

What course of action is open to the survivors or descendants of a collective identity defined by destruction? If all they can proffer is that destruction, and the loss of any way of bringing back to life the collective being that has vanished, then any action they may take, insofar as they are able to express demands, will go no further than calling for acknowledgement of the barbarity that their group has suffered, with material compensation according to the case. If, on the contrary, they are able to advance a positive principle, whatever that may be, the strands of a culture that still has a hope of revival, a view of justice for the society in which they live, a demand for democracy, then the community or group concerned can move forward. Here, an end to violence means creating a 'positive' identity, a principle that does not trap people in an identity which is 'negative' because it has been destroyed and belongs only to the past.

How can one rebuild in the case of the register of individual participation in modernity? Only a full and complete acknowledgement of that which has been prohibited or denied and the resulting wound can provide a satisfactory answer to the victims and those who claim to represent or embody them. The answer here is in the hands of those who hold the power to decide on such an acknowledgement, but who may have ideological or political reasons for not granting it. It may be a matter of protecting persecutors, avoiding re-opening very recent wounds, establishing or maintaining a precarious peace, going along with a consensus that has effected the transition from dictatorship to democracy relatively smoothly. Silence and obliviousness are generally justified by the overriding interests of the community; but they also obviously work in the interests of the persecutors and the guilty parties, to the detriment of the victims. The West German experience, for instance, especially from the 1960s on, suggests that a country which decided to undertake the work on itself required by a recent past of extreme acts of violence and mass crimes emerges better than a country which refuses to do so. Debating the past and developing a policy of truth and forgiveness, as South Africa tried to do after apartheid, is the best way of helping former victims to come back into the fold of the national community.

Lastly, can negation be reversed when the victims have been devastated as personal Subjects and deeply dehumanized? If their predominant feeling is that it is no longer possible for them to take back control of their lives and continue living, then the only outcome is a descent into madness or suicide. Among the worst of cases is that where the victims feel, after the event, that their own behaviour contributed to the negation of their own humanity, and that of others; that they play a part in their own debasement, which may spill over into a kind of inversion, being trapped inside a repugnant image of self which turns into a disgusting character that becomes their public image. Symmetrically it has been found – for example, from knowledge gathered about the Nazi concentration camp experience – that in conditions of extreme violence the resources provided by faith or by a previous political commitment increase the likelihood of remaining a Subject despite the dehumanizing environment, as well as making it more likely for the person to rebuild his or her subjectivity afterwards.

For the three registers of this analysis, the core of the end to violence is the same: it lies in the ability of the group, the individual, or the Subject to move forward. Irrespective of the register, three main attitudes are possible. The first of these involves shutting oneself up in the past, either in the barbarity experienced or in the time that preceded it, which will ultimately then be recalled as a golden age – before the disaster. In Sigmund Freud's terminology, this attitude is one of 'melancholy'. It may lead to demands for reparations, but is much less likely to evolve towards acknowledgement and forgiveness.

The second attitude, on the contrary, tries to forget the past, to distance oneself as much as possible from past history, either the period of extreme violence or before that, in an attempt to merge completely into the society or nation in which one lives. In this case, there can be no debate about the past.

Finally, the third attitude is to go through a period of 'mourning', again a Freudian concept, and to show that one is able to move forward and live fully in the society and in the nation, while still keeping alive the memory of the earlier experience and its destruction. The third attitude links the past, the present, and the future and is eminently favourable to opening up debate and processes of the 'truth and reconciliation' type that have developed throughout the world, in particular in Latin America, following the South African example initiated in 1993. This requires great moral and political strength on the part of its promoters. Nelson Mandela talked about this on a number of occasions, for example with Bill Clinton, who relates their conversation thus:

> I said, 'Madiba [Mandela's colloquial tribal name, which he asked me to use], I know you did a great thing in inviting your jailers to your inauguration, but didn't you really hate those who imprisoned you?' He replied, 'Of course I did, for many years. They took the best years of my life. They abused me physically and mentally. I didn't get to see my children grow up. Then one day when I was working in the quarry, hammering the rocks, I realized that they had already taken everything from me except my mind and my heart. Those they could not take without my permission. I decided not to give them away.' Then he looked at me, smiled, and said, 'And neither should you.'
> After I caught my breath, I asked him another question. 'When you were walking out of prison for the last time, didn't you feel the hatred rise up in you again?' 'Yes,' he said, 'for a moment I did. Then I thought to myself, they have had me for twenty-seven years. If I keep hating them, they will still have me. I wanted to be free, and so I let go.'[15]

Acknowledgement in a global world

Crimes against humanity, to confine ourselves to this particular form of violence, have taken place and still take place in arenas that do not necessarily coincide with the framework of modern-day states and nations. One immediate consequence is that the debates they many give rise to, and likewise their legal, political, and institutional processing, cannot therefore be restricted to that framework. In a 'Westphalian' world, the state provides continuity between the past and the future, and it is within the state that decisions on the granting of rights are made, the processes of political debate take place, steps towards reconciliation or forgiveness are taken, reparations are approved, and so on. This in no way excludes international processes or the institution of courts like the one at Nuremberg to try Nazi criminals after the Second World War – but such courts exist by virtue of an agreement between states.

However, acts of extreme violence, including those that took place in another age, often need to be analysed and dealt with at global level. Looking at the contemporary consequences of the slave trade from the victims' point of view, for example, means taking into account the historical dimension of the problem – nearly fifteen centuries – and considering the role of all sorts of players[16] in different parts of the world, in Africa, Asia, Europe, and the Americas. Thinking about the major so-called 'humanitarian' crises, the ethnic cleansing of the Great Lakes and the Balkans or the killings in Darfur, means bringing into focus processes inherent in Rwanda, former Yugoslavia, or Sudan and also, necessarily, regional and international, geopolitical, and economic dimensions. And if the survivors and descendants of the victims, some of whom have become refugees or exiles, are to emerge from such tragedies and rebuild their lives, that requires the involvement of many players, several of whom are external to the strictly local scene – humanitarian NGOs, international justice, international organizations like the UN or the EU, and so on.

What these survivors or descendants, the bearers, as Dipesh Chakrabarty[17] says, of 'historical wounds', may demand or hope for may involve the responsibility of several states, for acts for which not all of them are necessarily accountable; states, moreover, which may no longer exist or whose frontiers have greatly changed since the time of the acts of violence.

Today's players are not those of yesterday, yet accountability for the past is nevertheless likely to be unduly or wrongly laid at the door of one or other of them, so much so that many politicians now feel vexed by the demands for repentance that are made of them. The concept of descendant itself raises problems: how far can one postulate continuity down through the centuries in order to legitimately present oneself as a victim on the grounds of being a descendant of victims? The notion of survivor likewise deserves to be examined: in situations of extreme violence, why should they be representative of all the victims, as if they formed a homogeneous group?

Such questions make one's head spin, as Jacques Derrida[18] indeed showed with reference to forgiveness. How should one respond to the moral demand to forgive the unforgivable? It is neither straightforward nor easy to arrange forgiveness and make it meaningful in a situation where both victims and persecutors belong to the same nation-state and where perpetrators and direct survivors of extreme violence still live. And what should one do if those who can ask forgiveness are not guilty, but simply people in positions of power who personally are not culpable of any wrongdoing in connection with the violence? Or if those who can grant forgiveness are merely more or less distant descendants of the victims? Or if, moreover, the state is not the sole or even the main framework within which these questions should be asked? Was the state that was the Federal Republic of Germany in Cold War days more answerable for Nazism than that of the German Democratic Republic? Is the state of Israel entitled to represent the victims of the Shoah, and, if so, to what extent? Is it right for heads of state to forgive or to ask forgiveness in place of and on behalf of the victims, of all victims, including those not seeking forgiveness?

Dealing with the violent player: Subject policies?

Countering violence conventionally means linked policies of repression and prevention, either within the state framework (by mobilizing the police, the courts, schools, etc.), externally (diplomacy, war), or perhaps by combining the two dimensions. The latter is all the more necessary as globalization is blurring the points of reference, and the fight against organized crime and terrorism today, for example, calls for global strategies. We believe that our typology of the Subject of violence can make a useful contribution to developing these considerations.

If violence, at least in the dimensions that can be established, corresponds to the *Floating Subject*, that is to say, the difficulty or the impossibility of converting expectations or demands into action, then the most important thing is to establish or re-establish the conditions that allow conversion to take place. Such a proposition carries on very directly from the remarks made above about the opposition between violence and institutionalized conflict. It in fact means that the best strategy for reducing or preventing violence is to promote the training and development of social or political players responsible for the management – no matter how confrontational – of relations between them: the exact opposite of a breakdown in relations. At the global level, this means more and more players and institutions filling the supranational space all the time. At state level, it means forms of democracy that can resolve the contemporary crisis of political representation and allow the development and recognition of social and cultural players.[19]

The same idea applies on smaller scales. Within a company, for instance, the presence of powerful, well-organized trade unions, while often regarded as a source of problems by management, is in fact also and above all the management's best bulwark against the risks of a loss and breakdown of social or moral standards; union representatives are in fact a channel for bringing internal problems to light, avoiding the unspoken resentments that fuel a crisis, and negotiating; they also provide some predictability.

Refusing even to allow a framework for conflict to exist does not lead to order and peaceful industrial relations; it is more likely to promote crisis behaviour, starting with violence.

If violence concerns the *Hyper-Subject*, with its overabundance of meanings, it calls for symmetrical efforts. Here the problem is not one of a lack of meaning or of a framework for conflict; it has much more to do with the overload that turns a virtual conflict into war and violent breakdowns in relations. What those who can bring any influence to bear on the situation then have to do is to stop the dimensions corresponding to this meaning overload, be they ideological or religious, from over-determining action and preventing any debate or discussion, political or social process, or negotiation. Any intervention on their part is more likely to have some effect if it takes place at a very early stage, before the player has become so wrapped up in their own logic as to permit no concessions and to grant unqualified primacy to the absolute and radicalism.

The *Floating Subject* requires bottom-up strategies, from the absence of conflict and mediation towards the building or strengthening of confrontational relations. The *Hyper-Subject* requires the opposite, top-down strategies, back down from the meta-political to the political, from complete breakdown – notably religious – to debate and institutionalized conflict. A significant kind of intervention here may involve efforts to lend weight to those who, within the same ideology, or the same religion, can accept moderation, debate, and conciliation of their sense of identity with universal values of right and reason. This is the case, notably, in Western democracies whenever moderate Islam is respected and recognized there and is also encouraged not to allow Islamism to blight and weaken it.

Once they have embraced a mindset of radical purity, violent players are not generally likely to relinquish their beliefs and give up the 'all or nothing' that has become their way of thinking. The only way of ending violence in this case is, therefore, by force, repression, and calling in the army and the police.

It is hard to accept the hypothesis of the *Non-Subject*, for whom violence is meaningless, merely the expression of submission to a lawful authority. Such a hypothesis in fact takes away the violent player's sense of responsibility, turning him or her into an automaton, a bureaucrat untroubled by conscience in the service of a machine, someone acting without convictions or passions, who unquestioningly accepts the order or instruction to act. Let us give this hypothesis the benefit of the doubt, though; let us admit that there are some people or situations which it can explain. The only way to end violence here is to delegitimize the authority involved, or, at least, the practices concerned. The admittedly minor ordeals of 'ragging' new students, for example, were tolerated in France for a long time, being anchored in a 'tradition' itself rooted in certain educational establishments. It took energetic political intervention to delegitimize and ban ragging, and thus to make any continuing perpetrators aware of their responsibilities. Much more generally, anything in education which can raise the sense of individual and collective responsibility, conscience, the idea that the individual is accountable for his or her acts, can only serve to limit the space available for *Non-Subject* violence.

Cruelty and the violence of the *Anti-Subject* occur only in very specific conditions. They may, for example, accompany conventional warfare whenever a strong sense of impunity goes hand-in-hand with fear of the enemy, as was the case with the American forces facing the Japanese during the war in the Pacific[20] or during the Vietnam War (notably in the My Lai massacre, where 500 unarmed civilians were brutally killed by an American unit on 16 March 1968), or, to cite a recent example, at Abu Ghraib, in Iraq. Preventing cruelty means putting in place safeguards to prevent players from resorting to pure violence as an end in itself. This applies to the military authorities in time of war, who must not, in theory and according to the law of war, allow any meanings other than instrumental ones to attach to actions under their control and responsibility. It applies to those in charge of armed conflict organizations, who must avoid the dilution of meaning in relation to political ends that the recourse to pure violence implies for their members – unless pure violence is to be used as a means of terrorizing the enemy. And in the case of common cruelty, on the part of criminals, for example, this seems so remote from the problems that can be solved by conventional political responses that it requires different resources to combat it: repression admittedly, and education, but perhaps also religious, moral, or humanist values, of the kind referred to, for example, by Nelson Mandela at his meeting with Bill Clinton.

The violence of the *Survivor Subject*, as Jean Bergeret explains, is 'dominating and archaic'; it is based on a 'primitive fantasy that simply asks the question essential to the individual's survival: "The other person or me?" "Him or me?" "Survive or die?" "Survive at the risk of killing the other person?" '[21] The problem here is not an end to violence or, as Bergeret says, 'controlling violence'. It is a matter of knowing that those who resort to violence do not have the personal resources or the mental models to deal with the situations in which they find themselves. To Bergeret, juvenile violence, the anger and the hatred felt by France's 'suburban youth' (*jeunes des banlieues*) which come into this category, owe a lot to the shortcomings of adults, who are unable to provide them with suitable identity models.

Today, violence is a taboo. Perhaps the last one. This has not always been so, and not that long ago it even had a certain legitimacy, be it extolling revolution, supporting national liberation movements, showing understanding of terrorist groups, or identifying with guerrilla warfare. Rather than analysing it, intellectuals either supported it or opposed it, according to their political sympathies. The more it is held to be evil personified, the more violence appears meaningless to the point where, in its most decisive manifestations, it seems to be a product of barbarism or frenzy. The social sciences must not allow themselves to be swayed into accepting the hastily conceived ideas that reject violence without analysing it from the point of view of the inhuman, the incomprehensible, and the absurd. Yet, they must also resist the idea of giving meaning to destructive and sometimes self-destructive modes of behaviour. They must therefore tread carefully and acknowledge that any manifestation of violence, however insignificant, is linked to a meaning, but that link is twisted, perverted, is lost, or artificial. It is all the more difficult to follow that path given that the world in which we operate is no longer 'Westphalian'. Violence is a particularly stimulating challenge for the social sciences, as it forces the researcher to do a balancing act and to produce findings ranging from the most personal, private, and subjective to the most general, international, and global.

3

Global Terrorism

For the social sciences, terrorism is a minor subject; it was long considered something 'dirty' and neglected by researchers. There are several explanations for this which I think a long experience of research qualifies me to evoke here.[1]

Terrorism: something 'dirty'

Some explanations are related to the very working of the subjects concerned. As terrorism is not listed amongst the themes classically considered important, it has only rarely been included in the headings of dictionaries and other traditional volumes such as 'encyclopedias', 'textbooks', or state-of-the-art publications, and disciplinary conformism meant that it was not very attractive. Students who chose it for the subject of their thesis ran the risk of becoming marginalized in relation to the academic community in their subject and to be less well placed than others thereafter on the academic market – this risk being all the greater as terrorism is a problem which is at the crossroads of political science, history, sociology, even of law, and it is difficult to set it at the core of any one of these subjects. Those who are already recognized researchers who choose this subject – as was my case in the 1980s – run the risk of making themselves over-conspicuous in professional circles, of not obtaining the financing required for surveys, and, moreover, of falling prey to all sorts of misunderstanding and suspicions: peers wonder whether the researcher is not fascinated by the subject; those in power either wonder what sort of relation they have with the 'terrorists' or expect them to act as informants for the intelligence services; while the actors whom they study are always liable to endeavour to profit from the relation which the researcher is trying to establish with them. This is why, in the 1980s, as a French researcher, I avoided research subjects where my belonging to France would have exacerbated the difficulties. I studied extreme left terrorism in Italy instead of Action Directe, and the Basque separatism of ETA instead of Corsican nationalism.

Other explanations concern the phenomenon itself. For a considerable period of time, terrorism was perceived as an occasional phenomenon, something extraneous to the normal workings of society, possibly as a sort of curiosity, even if some of its manifestations did impress its contemporaries or, later on, some of the major thinkers: the Russian Populists who fascinated Albert Camus;[2] or the French anarchists at the end of the nineteenth and beginning of the twentieth century and the Macedonian, Armenian, Bosnian, and other nationals in the same period; extreme left groups and sometimes also, but more rarely, extreme right groups in several societies in the course of post-industrialization from the 1970s; Palestinian nationalists but also the Basques and the Irish in the same period, and so on. Experiences of this sort have given rise to countless texts, but they have only very rarely been considered first and foremost from the point of view of terrorism and analysed with the tools of the social sciences. Apart from journalists' texts, which tend to be dominated by a quest for the sensational, they have at best given rise to a series of 'expert' articles, reports, or books – a business which is particularly flourishing, for example, in the United States and especially in Washington, DC, where the think tanks, specialized journals, and consultants on this subject are legion, not to mention the official or semi-official services which specialize in anti-terrorism. A few respectable researchers have nevertheless at times produced useful texts on terrorism, such as the historian Walter Laqueur. But, on the whole, the best works, those which really contribute something fresh and serious, have long been those which touched on the theme of terrorism but did not make it their main subject, their prime interest being in phenomena of which it was a spin-off, an extreme, a specific dimension of a more general action – such as a national movement or a political struggle. If we take, for example, the bibliography of my book *The Making of Terrorism*,[3] it is easy to see that the most authoritative references are of this sort. Moreover, given the lack of any significant investment in the social sciences, it is perhaps in literature that we find the most illuminating texts on terrorism – one only has to read Dostoevsky to realize this.

Finally, if terrorism is something 'dirty', it is undoubtedly also because it refers to forms of action which are themselves 'dirty' and to which correspond methods of political and repressive action themselves often unsavoury, even in democracies. The term 'terrorism' is in fact extremely negative; there is nothing noble about it and it is even often used to deride, if not criminalize, those to whom it is applied. The only period in which the players themselves have at times used this term to refer to themselves, and with no qualms, is that of the Russian Populists and their social-revolutionary extensions. Thus Vera Zasulich, who had injured a Russian officer known for his brutality towards prisoners, declared to the jury (which, moreover, acquitted her): 'I am not a criminal, I am a terrorist.' Twenty years later, Boris Savinkov – a social-revolutionary leader in early twentieth-century Russia – described himself as a terrorist as we can read in his very interesting *Memoirs of a Terrorist*.[4]

The discrediting associated with the use of the term 'terrorism' makes of it an everyday category which it is not easy to transform into a sociological category. A transformation of this type is even more difficult to implement given that the very image of the terrorist is usually that of a barbarian, someone insane or with a pathological personality – which periodically various pseudo-scientific studies vainly endeavour to prove. Describing it in other terms – for example, by seeking meaning behind the apparent insanity – is to come up against an instant consensus which massively rejects any approach to understanding – is it not common parlance to say that any attempt to understand and explain terrorism is to justify it?

Nevertheless in symposiums or specialized studies, reference is frequently made to a fundamental difficulty which it is impossible to resolve, namely that those who are terrorists for some are freedom fighters or resistants for others. But in fact this is another way of eluding a scientific approach to the phenomenon and precluding any satisfactory definition.

The transition from everyday language to a scientific vocabulary is a particularly delicate operation here and one which implies a capacity for distancing and reflexivity which it is difficult to encourage. The fact is that, at least until the 1990s, one of the specificities of terrorism was that it only came to the forefront in sporadic fashion. When it was not a period of intense terrorist activity there was no social or political demand for it to be studied and researchers were not encouraged to take an interest in it. When bombs were exploding or attacks being made, aeroplanes being hijacked or kidnappings on the increase, the researcher, questioned by the media or even by political authorities, was summoned to explain the issues, here and now, and therefore to act as an expert; an occurrence much more frequent than any invitation to take some distance from the events, to analyse the lengthy processes culminating in this extreme violence, or to consider the scope of the term 'terrorism'. Moreover, the anti-terrorist action of the authorities, which is usually accompanied by very intense attention from the media, encourages the proliferation of specialists whose competence is at times open to doubt. This results in academic production being drowned in floods of specialized literature – usually of mediocre quality – and which discredits it; all that glitters is not gold. Journalists surfing on the crest of the news; experts informed by secret service agents; lawyers, magistrates, or politicians who all tend to manipulate the facts and who themselves get their information from journalists and specialists; writers who are more concerned with ideology than with the desire to produce documented, indepth knowledge: all sorts of actors contribute to making 'terrorism' an object which appears to belong to others rather than to social science researchers. Jean-Paul Brodeur has observed this and stated that it is preferable to characterize as 'theatrical' rather than something 'dirty' this type of phenomenon which gives rise to passionate interest from the public when it occurs, with a drama unfolding on a symbolic level and provoking, as he explains, a desire for catharsis which prevails over any interest in knowledge.[5]

All this only goes to reinforce the idea that, in the last resort, as far as terrorism is concerned, those who know do not speak and those who do speak know nothing. We might add a further remark which stems from the very functioning of the anti-terrorist discourse: as I saw for myself when doing research in Washington, DC, in the mid-1980s, antiterrorism is in fact a set of proposals which are the outcome of the interplay of all sorts of actors, pressure groups, governmental agencies, media, and so on, whose interests are very far from being restricted uniquely to the fight against this particular form of violence. Understanding what is said about terrorism and about the way in which it should be countered in a given society may therefore involve attempting to understand how this society functions and not only analysing terrorism properly speaking.[6]

The concept of terrorism

But today terrorism seems to be a permanent feature, as a threat and, often, as a reality which is sufficiently important to justify systematic consideration in which the social sciences must play their part. To confront a challenge of this sort, it is appropriate that it ceases to be a minor and somewhat 'dirty' object. Now it would in no way suffice to propose serious and well-documented historical analyses; it is essential to go to the core of the theoretical difficulties which hinder the understanding of terrorism and to formulate a concept of it.

This concept must enable us to go beyond the impasse which consists at the outset in considering any judgement of a 'terrorist' experience as relative, recalling that while there are those who perceive it as such, there are others who deny this and who, on the contrary, valorize its violence. In fact, this state of mind functions by amalgamating two elements of definition which it is urgent to distinguish analytically, even if it means thereafter articulating them in the concrete approach to 'terrorist' experiences. Terrorism must be approached, on one hand, from the angle of the methods to which it has recourse and, on the other, from that of the meaning which it expresses but, as we shall see, which it also corrupts.

In one way, terrorism can be grouped under instrumental action: it can be defined as the implementation of tools and resources at a modest cost in comparison to the effects expected by its promoters. Is it not possible, for example, for a terrorist group with a few handguns or a few kilos of explosives to destabilize a regime, end a government, in short to obtain results out of all proportion to the means used? This first part of the definition of terrorism has the merit of stressing its highly rational character. The actors here are capable of elaborating a strategy, of calculating, of equipping themselves with instruments within their reach and, if necessary, creating difficulties for a state which is infinitely more powerful than they are. They may appear to be more intelligent in this respect than the governments which they confront. Thus, while for years American strategists had been drawing up very sophisticated approaches and imagining particularly elaborate scenarios of nuclear, chemical, or bacteriological terrorism, the authors of the attacks on 11 September 2001 went up in airliners after having acquired the rudiments of flying, their only weapons being penknives or Stanley knives. Facing up to states with military and police

forces at their disposal, terrorism, in its instrumental dimension, makes use of a limited range of easily acquired, inex-
pensive tools, readily available in civil society. Each group
or each organization has its own repertoire, which often acts
as its signature in the eyes of the specialists responsible for
identifying the authors of an attack or the hijacking of a
plane. Speaking of terrorist methods cannot be a question
of drawing up a list of techniques, since they vary from one
experience to another; it involves primarily stressing a dis-
proportion, an extraordinary asymmetry, since the mobilization of modest means will enable terrorists to confront or
to get at governments endowed with the most powerful
resources possible.

In many respects, technological change facilitates the task
of terrorist actors today. With the internet, they have access
to information, for example, about how to construct fatal
instruments; they can communicate with each other or
indulge in activities of proselytism and propaganda to the
point that people refer to 'Wiki-Qaeda', 'e-jihad', and 'Cyber
Islamism'. In the past, states had technological[7] and scientific
resources which were not accessible to private individuals,
whereas today actors in civil society have access to a huge
market of products and knowledge – this feeds the fears of
seeing the implementation of 'bioterrorism' and other threats
of this type.[8]

Rational instrumentality is not unknown to the world of
terrorists. Here we still have to introduce a recent element,
but one which complicates the analysis of this dimension of
the phenomenon: the rise in suicide attacks. For, when the
terrorist does more than risk his life, when he gives it, with
no reservations, and when this is, at least in part, a personal
decision, it then becomes difficult to speak of a modest
investment, disproportionate to the results expected. Here,
rationality can no longer be the object of a cost/benefit type
of analysis, except to consider that the choice of suicide
operations and the decision of martyrdom can be attributed
not to those who are going to kill themselves, but to the
leaders of organizations who manipulate or instrumentalize

individuals ready to kill themselves. Now, even if the vast majority of Islamist suicide operations do imply an organized process,[9] research – as we shall see – does not allow us to systematically and exclusively take as read this scenario of heteronomy and lack of meaning for those individuals who are going to kill themselves.

This brings us directly to consider the second dimension constituent of terrorism, which is its relation to meaning. Those viewpoints which reduce the phenomenon to its sole dimensions of instrumental violence – that is, of means to an end – should never lead us to forget that the terrorist act, from the protagonist's viewpoint, does have a meaning. Whether the actors express a view or not, for them their action is loaded with meanings. The specificity of these meanings is that they are always different from what they would be if they were not implemented violently. In terrorism, resorting to violence is always accompanied by distortions or deviations as compared with the meaning of the same action without using weapons, explosives, and so on.

In some cases, an ideology stands in for the loss of meaning, with the terrorist acting because the meaning escapes him and he wishes to maintain it artificially. Thus, for example, in the 1970s and 1980s, Italy experienced a wave of extreme-left terrorism exclusively linked to the working-class movement although this movement was on the decline, losing its historical centrality, and the workers in no way identified with this violence. The more the distance increased between the figure of reference – the proletariat – and the discourse claiming to continue to personify this figure at the topmost level of the revolution, the more the bearers of this discourse tended to get carried away into unlimited violence. This loss of meaning can result in the nihilism of the 'demons' which Dostoevsky describes so well. But one should be cautious here and not tack this schema over-hastily onto the facts: André Glucksmann, the philosopher, was mistaken when he interpreted the '9/11' attacks in the light of this model for, in this instance, there was a plethora of meaning rather than a lack of meaning in the violence.[10]

In other cases, the violence accompanies a rationale of overload of meaning, in which the actors attribute a religious and metaphysical signification to their political and social expectations. This is the case in the terrorism associated with radical Islamism.

In yet other cases, what we see is the inability to continue reconciling elements of meaning which previously could function together without major difficulties. Thus, ETA, the Basque separatist organization, came to the fore under Franco and not only voiced the hopes of those who wished to liberate the (Basque) nation from oppression under Franco, by ending the political dictatorship, but also expressed the expectations of a working class which, at the time, was numerous, but severely repressed. At this point, the violence of ETA was limited and, above all, symbolic. Then democracy was established, the Basque nation obtained a vast degree of autonomy, and de-industrialization put an end to the centrality of working-class struggles. It was at this point that the violence of ETA took a genuinely, sometimes unbridled terrorist turn, the only way of keeping alive the myth of an action speaking at one and the same time in the name of an oppressed nation, a proletariat forbidden to express itself, and a mobilization against the repression of the Spanish state – allegedly democratic but in appearance only.

Ideology, religion, or myth: in the three cases violence is one of the aspects of the *Hyper-Subject* presented in the previous chapter.

Sometimes the terrorist act includes, or unleashes, dimensions of gratuitous violence or sadism, totally unrelated to the meaning of the action and which in no way further it – for example, when the guards of people who have been kidnapped and who will be liberated in exchange for a ransom submit these people to cruel and humiliating treatment. The *Anti-Subject* is to be found in some terrorist experiences, but it is not central thereto. It is still true to say that terrorism is a special type of political violence. Its political issues are continually shored up, indeed invaded by, processes of both loss and meaning overload which lead it either towards infra-political forms of behaviour, in which the dominant element becomes economic, even dissolute, close to organized crime, for example, or else towards meta-political forms of behaviour in which the dominant element goes beyond the political and even, for religion, beyond life on earth.

The less meaning is lost, or distant, in relation to what it would be without the resort to violence, the more the latter appears as instrumental and the less it is justified to speak in terms of terrorism. Terrorism, therefore, is seen in all its conceptual purity when, on the contrary, it no longer maintains any link with the real world, with a social, national, cultural, or political figure of reference which could identify with its acts. Terrorism conforms to its concept in extreme, perhaps even exceptional, cases, where only its protagonist is likely to be able to confer legitimate meaning on its action and where no figure of reference whatever can identify with it. In all other cases, it is 'impure', imperfect, and incomplete. When Al-Qaeda organized the '9/11' attacks, it evoked revulsion all over the world, but also applause – explicit to varying degrees – amongst the Muslim masses in some countries: in these instances, it is not possible to speak of 'pure' terrorism. When the Italian Red Brigades killed bosses or political leaders in the name of a working class which rejected their violence and when, apart from their members, they no longer had any symbolic or ideological recognition, they became truly terrorist – moreover, it was at this point that they became weaker and vulnerable to the repression which put an end to their experience.

The definition of 'pure' terrorism may appear to lead to a paradox. For, whereas in reality the phenomenon is of a political nature, we are proposing a 'pure' concept which departs from the political. This concept is in fact the extreme point of the phenomenon, its outcome when the processes of loss and overload of meaning enter their terminal phase, departing from reality, when violence turns in upon itself and is no longer uniquely a problem of armed repression in the face of individuals or groups who proclaim their own legitimacy for lack of the least social, cultural, or political legitimacy. But in practice the phenomenon is almost always 'impure'; it almost always retains a contact, even very limited, with a population of reference, a social reality, pockets of sympathy or understanding, and it is this 'impurity' in practice which means that it remains political.

Classical terrorism

As a historical reality, terrorism resembles many other social or political phenomena in that there have been considerable changes since the period between 1960 and 1980. To be more precise: it has gone from the classical era to the global era. Some observers challenge this image of a distinct change or break. Hans Magnus Enzensberger, for example, while not playing down the innovations introduced by radical Islamism, which has, as he says, 'replaced the omniscient and all-powerful central Committee by a flexible network', insists on recalling that 'modern terrorism is a European invention dating from the nineteenth century. ... Recently,' he adds, 'its main source of inspiration has been the extreme-left terrorism of the 1960s and 1970s.'[11] He considers that the techniques of the Islamists, their symbols, the style of their communiqués, and so on, borrow massively from the extreme-left groups of the past. One might add, to follow him for an instant, that the practice of suicide is not a novelty in terrorism. Terrorists at the end of the nineteenth and beginning of the twentieth century took risks which verged on suicide to approach their target with a bomb, a pistol, or a knife. Bobby Sands in 1981 and other IRA members, Ulrike Meinhof in 1976, Andreas Baader in 1977, and other members of the Red Army Faction all committed suicide in prison – though it is true that their act involved no other deaths but their own.

The fact remains that Enzensberger himself, a few lines further on in the book referred to, weakens the hypothesis of historical continuity by noting that Islamist terrorists 'are in reality pure products of the globalized world which they combat' and that 'in comparison with their predecessors they have made a lot of progress, not only in the techniques they employ, but in their use of the media'.[12] While it would be absurd to postulate a complete break, it does still seem more relevant to highlight the elements of transition from one era to another rather than those which indicate a degree of continuity. This transition can be observed materially by analysing the forms and meanings terrorism assumed yesterday and comparing them to those of the present day. There have also been considerable changes in the categories we can now use to consider this phenomenon.

In the period from 1960 to 1980, terrorism was in the main the concern of the analytical framework of the nation-state and its extension, international relations. Within the nation-state – or at least within sovereign states – it corresponded to three major headings. It could be extreme-left, extreme-right, or nationalist and separatist.

By far the most widespread expression of extreme-left terrorism was played out in Italy, but it affected numerous other societies in varying degrees of industrialization: West Germany with the Red Army Faction and the Revolutionary Cells; France with Action Directe; Japan with its Red Army; Belgium with the Revolutionary Communist Cells; Greece, Portugal, and so on. It originated in what I then called an *inversion* in which the protagonists of violence, in the deviation of post-1968 leftism, appropriated the categories of Marxism–Leninism, altered them to suit themselves, and then spoke in the name of a proletariat, or others, which they in no way represented. On each occasion, they challenged the power of the state, even if in some cases they did try to be international and establish themselves in a space other than national and if they did vigorously denounce American imperialism. Extreme-right terrorism was not as widespread, but was also borne along by projects for the seizure of state power and was linked to the presence, in the machinery of the states concerned, of sectors which were themselves open to such projects. Finally, and still internal to sovereign states, terrorism could be the modus operandi of nationalist movements wishing to impose the independence of a nation; with the use of violence being a means of reviving such aspirations if need be. In Europe the Basque and the Irish movements were thus characterized by resorting to armed struggle and by comparable forms of organization, in particular with the same type of tug of war between 'military' and warlike rationales and 'political' approaches more open to negotiation.

Furthermore, international terrorism was for the most part the doing of actors claiming to support the Palestinian cause, either as their main feature – for example, with the killing of the Israeli athletes perpetrated by Fatah in 1972 in the Olympic village in Munich – or incidentally, with in these instances the intervention of groups which tended to be manipulated by 'sponsor' states (Syria, Libya, Iraq, etc.) and attempting to weaken the central rationale of the PLO and preventing any negotiated solution in the Israeli–Palestinian conflict. The ASALA (Armenian Secret Army for the Liberation of Armenia) resembled in some respects the Palestinian groups on which it was modelled all the more so as, like them, in crisis-ridden Lebanon it found a territory propitious to its brief prosperity.

The characteristic of classical terrorism, that of the period from 1960 to 1980, was that it was active within a 'Westphalian' world – a world which it was possible and legitimate to approach in the categories which Ulrich Beck calls 'methodological nationalism'.[13] Terrorism originated within societies which themselves lay within states; it conveyed political and ideological deviations which referred back to projects either for taking power in a state or to setting up a state, and it was borne by avant-gardes who identified with the direction of history, the working class, and the nation. And, symmetrically, the struggle against terrorism was an affair in which each state was involved uniquely for its own benefit – which did not preclude appeals to international solidarity. Classical terrorism was perceived and described as a threat affecting states, their order, and, possibly, their territorial integrity.

Global terrorism

The '9/11' attacks revealed what it was possible to glimpse, in fact, almost ten years before: the entry into the 'global' era of terrorism. This era had in fact been inaugurated by various episodes conveyed by radical Islamism, with in particular the first attempt at an Islamist attack in New York in 1993, which even then targeted the towers of the World Trade Center, or yet again the hijacking of an Air France plane in Algeria in December 1994 by Islamists whose project was to crash the plane over Paris. This hijacking was itself followed a few months later by a series of attacks in France which were part of the same 'global' rationale since they combined international dimensions (the extension of the Algerian Islamist struggle outside the national space of Algeria) and dimensions internal to French society (crisis in the *'banlieues'* [poor high-rise out-of-town developments], social exclusion, the experience of racism internalized and turned into violence).

One can even go farther back in time and find the beginnings of global terrorism in the attacks in which a suicide bomber driving a delivery van destroyed the American embassy in Beirut (April 1983), then the attack on the headquarters of the French contingent of the multinational security force and the American marines barracks bombing (October 1983). These are, according to the most likely hypotheses, the first expressions of Hezbollah, a movement which claimed to be borne by the project for an Islamic revolution throughout the region, and which also intended to finish with the State of Israel, and which from this time onwards was capable of mobilizing people destined to commit suicide in their actions.

The fact remains that the globalization of terrorism was demonstrated in spectacular fashion with the attacks on 11 September 2001. With these attacks the phenomenon can no longer be analysed in the categories of 'methodological nationalism' as the classical limits between rationales internal to sovereign states and the external, so-called international, rationales had become blurred. The authors of the '9/11' attacks moved around in a global space; their careers took them from the society in which they were born, Saudi Arabia and Egypt in this instance, to other societies, like Sudan, Pakistan, and Afghanistan, where they met, were educated and trained, creating bonds of solidarity which were to become active in the form of networks throughout the world and where they had the benefit of complete freedom of action on the part of the state of the Taliban, whom they had subjugated. They were at home in several countries in Europe, including Germany, where some of them attended university, in the England of 'Londonistan' and its mosques, where the most radical speechifying went unchecked, as well as in the French suburbs. These actors, contrary to what is usually assumed, were not the expression of a real-life, somewhat traditional community from which they might have emerged giving direct expression to their expectations, but on the contrary were people who had been uprooted and were very far from any such community. They came from a *transnational neo-umma*, in the words of Farhad Khosrokhavar, an imagined community which tends to be formed in the poor areas of the major global cities in the modern world rather than in traditional rural areas.[14] In their action, there were rationales which were reminiscent of those of the most modern capitalism possible – it has even been stated that Bin Laden, the leader of Al-Qaeda, was guilty of 'insider trading' when speculating on the Stock Exchange about the consequences of the attacks that his organization was preparing.

Actors of this type function in networks with considerable flexibility; they know how to connect and disconnect without difficulty and, given their instrumental rationality, they use the most advanced technologies of communication, beginning with the internet. Their terrorism is also global as a result of its meanings, which are not restricted to taking power in a state or separating from it. Their aims are global and even extend beyond the world in which we live, being projected into the after-life. Breaking with the traditional forms of community life, their Islamism – inseparable from the concept of *jihad* (holy war) – transcends national frontiers and aims at the destruction of the West, including by martyrdom and therefore a sacred death; this West which both fascinates them and, in their opinion, excludes and despises Islam and Muslims.

The attacks on 11 September 2001 were not the first expression, likely in future to be surpassed, of this terrorism expressed by transnational actors but a paroxysm, an extreme case. Thereafter, numerous attacks were made in the name of Al-Qaeda, or at least associated with this organization, but they did not present the same transnational purity – in other words, there was a blending of global-level dimensions with others, more classically set in the framework of the state being targeted. Moreover, it is to these hybrid expressions which articulate world-level, supranational aspects with internal aspects of the states concerned that the idea of a globalization of terrorism applies the best. Whether it be a question of the attacks in Riyadh, Casablanca, and Istanbul in 2003, those in Madrid (March 2004) or yet again in London (July 2005), in each instance the actors articulate, in ways which vary from one instance to another, the two dimensions which constitute 'global' terrorism. On one hand they are at one and the same time, at least in part, and at least for some of them, embedded in the society in which they act, the end product there of the logic of social exclusion and lack of respect; they express an acute feeling of not finding their place in this society or, yet again, they convey a rejection of its international politics. On the other hand, they are bearers of transnational, religious rationales and, if need be, are linked to global-level networks. Consequently they concern simultaneously an imagined community of believers with no material base and a real-life community, for example of Moroccan immigrants (Spain) or Pakistanis (England) or yet again the poverty-stricken masses living in the most deprived areas of Casablanca or Istanbul. Their action is neither uniquely internal nor classical, nor uniquely transnational, but both at the same time. This, moreover, is why the answers to this 'global' terrorism themselves combine two dimensions: military and defence dimensions vis-à-vis the outside world, on one hand, and police and internal security, on the other.

In some instances, the transnational dimension itself is slight, even non-existent, and the terrorist action is in the main limited to its classical dimensions. This is the case with the suicide attacks committed by Palestinians against targets in Israel. The practice of martyrdom is an innovation in Palestinian action which has only recently become Islamist. But above all, this violence emanates directly from a real-life community, the populations of the territories placed under the control of the Palestinian Authority, and the references to Islam remain subordinate to the national struggle. The transnational dimensions of the action are of little import and, if it is possible to speak of terrorism, it must be recognized that the latter remains classical and not global.

'Global' terrorism is deployed in a space which is therefore edged by two extreme limits. At one extreme it is purely transnational – this was the case with the 11 September 2001 attacks; at the other extreme, it is classical, as least when it is a question of its frame of reference – this is the case with the Palestinian attacks in Israeli territory.

Is this global terrorism entirely new? In the past, the classical age of the phenomenon, numerous actors had transnational trajectories, cut off from any rooting in their society of origin. The three Japanese who opened fire at the airport of Lod in Israel on 30 May 1972 (twenty-six dead) had come to serve the Palestinian cause, just as, throughout the 1970s, the Germans of the Revolutionary Cells, the Movement 2 June, or the Red Army Faction collaborated with terrorist Palestinian groups, or with the 'sponsor' states. In these instances there was effectively deterritorialization, on one hand, and networking of all these actors, on the other. But it was more a question of international support for a national cause than of a global action. The violence was intended to be on behalf of the Palestinian movement; the existence of the networks, which numerous experts described as a common theme or 'leitmotif', was uniquely due to the support or the tolerance of certain states.

Is global terrorism the monopoly of radical Islamism? It is true that terrorist actors other than Muslims do exist today throughout the world and that many armed movements, whether nationalist, ethnic, or borne by another religion (Hinduism, for example), use them. But radical Islamism is the only one to combine global, meta-political aims, and possible roots within a sovereign state in various parts of the world. As a result, there is less room left for violent, other than Islamist, actors, as was observed in spectacular fashion in Spain. The terrible attacks on 11 March 2004 in Madrid (191 people killed) were first attributed by the government to ETA before it became clear that they were the work of Maghrebian immigrants. Not only did José Maria Aznar's Partido Popular lose the elections which were held a few days later for having erroneously accused ETA, but the Basque separatist organization itself was in a way a victim of Islamic terrorism and was also obliged to impugn such extreme violence; henceforth its legitimacy in the use of arms and explosives was weakened. This is why we can say that, by its intervention in Spain, Al-Qaeda signified the historical decline of ETA – even if this organization continues to exist and to deal murderous blows to Spanish democracy.

But let us add here that Islamist terrorism is not unified or homogeneous – far from it. Resorting to extreme violence claiming to represent Islam mobilizes actors who become involved in highly conflictual games amongst themselves, as we see today in Iraq, where Al-Qaeda is far from having the monopoly of attacks.

More generally, if we consider classical terrorism, that of the 1960s and 1970s, one can see an image of a tendency to split. Yesterday's rationales were primarily political, obsessed, as we said, by seizing state power or by the establishment of a new state. In the present-day world, in comparison with the classical age, terrorist action is either *more than political*, overdetermined by its dimensions of sacred global combat, with no possibility of negotiation – radical Islamism reigns here, it is *meta-political*; or else it is *less than political*, concerned in these cases with economic profit while maintaining contact with the political. This, for example, is the case in Colombia with the FARC, who have become *infra-political* forces, today on the decline. This either brings the actual phenomenon closer to the concept of 'pure' terrorism or else, on the contrary, moves it farther away, making of it a primarily instrumental and economic type of violence with a tendency to Mafia-like practices. This evolution does not preclude the existence of nationalist or comparable movements, still liable to resort, classically, to terrorism but of necessity confined and reduced to their local issues.

The subjectivity of victims and of perpetrators

Traditionally, apart from rapidly expressing our regrets, little attention was paid to the victims of terrorism. The dead were counted while, in the main, nothing was known about the wounded and the traumatized. Practically no provisions were made for care, in either the immediate or long term. Once the emotion had subsided, after an attack or a hijacking, there was almost no acknowledgement of those whom the extreme violence had left suffering, destitute, and often alone. Terrorism was primarily a problem for the state involved, for its politics and diplomacy, so much so that in the name of reasons of state, particularly when international terrorism was concerned and even in the most advanced democracies, it was impossible to ensure that serious inquiries were carried out to completion and that the courts really and fully did their work. 'Twelve years after the hijacking of the Airbus 300 [which left Algiers in December 1994 and is cited above] we do not know the true protagonists, or the people behind it [. . .]. I know, I check it each time, reasons of State prevent any inquiry. Even for the terrible attacks in 1986,' explains Françoise Rudetzki, the founder of the NGO

SOS Attentats-SOS Terrorisme, 'the "small fry" have been tried, Tunisian underlings, whereas those who gave the orders, the Iranians who are really to blame, have never been troubled.'[15]

But today, thanks precisely to the mobilization of people like Françoise Rudetzki, who created her association in 1983, after the attack on the Le Grand Véfour restaurant in Paris, in which she was seriously wounded, victims have begun to be recognized, compensated in France by a guarantee fund set up by law, taken charge of immediately, in their psychological state of suffering, and, more than in the past, pressure from public opinion forces the legal system to carry out full inquiries. Now, as Françoise Rudetzki very correctly points out, 'recognition by the law is essential to enable the victims to reconstruct themselves. The trial is the final phase which will enable them to emerge from the painful, uncomfortable status of victim, which at times induces feelings of guilt.'[16]

As the reader of this book already knows, this evolution is part of the much broader tendency of contemporary societies to take an interest in people, and groups, affected by violence in their physical or intellectual integrity, individually or collectively, in the present or in the past of which they retain the stigmata. It constitutes the first aspect of the entry in force of the Subject in thought and analysis concerning terrorism.

The second aspect relates to the terrorists themselves. Classically, as we have seen, their subjectivity is usually ignored by the analysis, which either reduces it to their calculations, their instrumental rationality, or else is at pains to demonstrate the pathological nature of the terrorist personality. In my research in the 1980s, I had begun to be very critical of this tendency and had even suggested reversing the remarks made spontaneously: it is the prolonged experience of living clandestinely, of life in small groups shut in on themselves, of the practice of armed struggle, and of the right which one assumes to dispose of the life of others which shape the potential terrorist personality. This is not so much a starting point and therefore an explanatory element of violent action as a finishing line, the consequence of drifting off-course which has ended in the practice of violence. But the present-day generalization of suicide attacks forces us to go much further in our thinking about the subjectivity of terrorist actors, even if numerous specialists do their utmost to think of the Islamic suicide attack as primarily being in the category of instrumental, tactical, calculated action[17] – a mode of approach which may be relevant if it is a question of the organizations involved, but which ceases to be so if it is a question of individuals, of whom it is difficult to see what type of cost/benefit calculations they could be envisaging.

In the first instance the issue is the rejection of an elementary form of sociology. For, contrary to a stereotype, the most radical Islamists, those who are closest to personifying global terrorism and who are ready to give their lives, are not necessarily from the poorest circles socially, nor are they deprived. They too belong to the educated middle classes, as the British discovered, to their great astonishment, at the time when they learned that the failed attacks in London (29 and 30 June 2007) had been prepared by doctors. They are Muslims – sometimes converts – who know the West well because they live there, or have lived there or at least have been confronted with it, if only through the media. They do not constitute a homogeneous set of people, and, if they do, they share important features – the very keen feeling of humiliation which they wish to end, hatred of the Jews, the conviction of being at war with the West. It is nevertheless possible on the basis of the subjectivity of each individual to distinguish several major types of actors. Thus Farhad Khosrokhavar suggests distinguishing four types of *jihadis*, whom he names Islamo-nihilist, Islamo-plethorist, Islamo-individualist, and Islamo-fundamentalist.[18] This researcher is remarkably well placed since he has studied young Muslims in French '*banlieues*', Muslim detainees in British prisons, and elsewhere in Europe, but also in revolutionary Iran and Islam in various Middle Eastern countries.

In a previous book he queried: 'how are we to understand the death wish of these groups of men who are willing to be slain and who also aspire to slaying others?'[19] His explanation is as follows: the transition to the 'global' martyr is implemented primarily in instances where the modernity of the city and the absence of bearings create amongst migrants a feeling of loss of self, and of helplessness, and promote the project of a globalized form of Islam. The combination of difficulties in participating in modernity and the feeling of being confronted with a brusque refusal of Islam results in an explosive mixture of revolt and hatred.

As soon as one adopts this type of approach, terrorists construct their subjectivity in the course of an unusual experience, along a path on which they are confronted with a globalized world and one in which they feel exposed, particularly in the global city described by Saskia Sassen[20] – which reinforces the validity of the adjective 'global' we attribute to it. Marc Sageman, who has built up a corpus of data relating to 394 Salafi terrorists, also insists on the diasporic nature of this experience (84 per cent joined the *jihad* in a country other than the one in which they were born). He observes that they are, on the whole, educated; many have qualifications in technical fields (medicine, architecture, engineering, information technology, business); three-quarters are 'professionals' (physicists, lawyers, engineers, teachers) or 'semi-professionals' (businessmen, IT specialists, etc.); and very few have had a true religious education. In the words of this psychiatrist, who was long associated with the CIA, it was 'this combination of technical education and lack of religious sophistication that made them vulnerable to an extreme interpretation of Islam'.[21] Sageman, in a manner which resembles Khosrokhavar's research, sets out a typology of trajectories which lead to *jihad* and lists seven types. There also, the actors are defined by their subjectivity and their attempt to constitute themselves as actors, giving meaning to their experience. Like Khosrokhavar, he wonders what makes them want to kill civilians and kill themselves at the same time. He stresses the social dynamics at work amongst the *jihadis*, their feeling of moral superiority, their belief in a collective future; he discusses change in values – from the secular to the religious, from the immediate to the long term, from traditional morality to new morality – and, there again, the intensity of hatred of Jews.

Approaches of this type tackle the question of subjectivization and de-subjectivization; it is their dialectic which leads to terrorism and martyrdom. These approaches reveal the sources of commitment, the existential meaning assumed by belief, the extent of the demonization of the West and of anti-Semitism. Here terrorists are reduced neither to some form of social role, possibly even a type, nor to their calculations, decisive as these may be. Nor are they reduced to the indoctrination or the manipulation implemented by the organization which sends them to their death, as if they had no personal reason for acting, as if they were not Subjects. To understand their action, we are thus invited to take an interest in them as Subjects, to try to get to know and understand their intentions, representations, and religiosity.

We can conclude this chapter with the same observation as in the preceding chapter. The sociology of 'global' terrorism is in fact only one rather specific domain of the sociology of violence. It has to accomplish a similar task – link elements which at first sight seem to be totally unrelated. These are, on one hand, the major changes in the world, transnational processes, and the way in which these synchronize with more restricted processes because they are deeply rooted in the framework of states; and, on the other, the subjectivity of the actors, which affects their most personal aspects, their most private personal experiences, their dreams and their despair. These links, which involve a delicate balancing act, are possible and necessary quite simply because the subjectivity of the actors, the way in which they construct themselves mentally, in which they produce their personal and collective imagined world, owes a lot to their exposure to the most global modernity, their belonging to but also their peregrinations in the universe of globalization which fascinates them and rejects them at one and the same time.

4

The Return of Racism

We are no longer in the 1950s or 1960s when the hope of seeing racism decline prevailed and the movements for civil rights and the processes of decolonization were advancing. On the contrary, present-day modernity, like yesterday, still has this dark side. And not only does this devastating phenomenon tend to persist in social life, but the ongoing changes provide resources for the reorganization of its operations in forms some of which are traditional and others new or altered. New racist actors are emerging while the old ones have not completely disappeared; new racist discourses and new racist practices are forging their way alongside older ones. After the discovery of the Nazi crimes, one might have thought that there was no longer a platform from which anti-Semitism could express itself. Yet this highly specific figure of hatred of the Other is once again launching forth, also fed in many respects by the passions which, throughout the world, surround anything to do with Israel and the Israeli–Palestinian conflict.[1]

The problem is global, but each region of the world and even each country has its own specific version; this is why comparative studies are of considerable interest in this subject.[2] Confronted with this restructuring, the social sciences are in search of new analytical tools, and new categories are taking shape for considering evil in its historical continuity as well as in its renewed forms.

Initial changes: the years 1970 to 1990

At the end of the 1960s in the context of the effects of the movement for civil rights in the United States and the radicalization towards violence of the Black movement, in particular following the brutal repression of the Black Panthers, the acknowledgement of the persistence of racism in the first instance involved asking: how is it that racism against black Americans survives, including in instances where nobody, or almost nobody, any longer dares to describe themselves as openly racist?

Institutional racism

At the time, the Black Power militants Stokely Carmichael and Charles Hamilton[3] were amongst the first to advance an explanation: racism is institutional – that is, it constitutes a structural characteristic of the system, even if the actors do not describe themselves as racists and would often be very astonished if they were accused of being so. From this point of view, ultimately nobody is racist but nevertheless black people are still victims of all sorts of discrimination.

Is institutional racism not a structural reality of contemporary democracies in which nobody dares to admit openly to being racist and where, in many situations, nobody has to assume responsibility for any sort of racism yet discrimination proves to be at work as soon as one makes the effort to reveal it openly? At first sight, the answer would appear to be in the affirmative. Thus, in an action-research study which he carried out with the French Democratic Confederation of Labour (CFDT), Philippe Bataille demonstrated how a firm of six hundred employees was able to avoid employing a single immigrant in an economically stricken town, Alès, in which the immigrant population represented roughly a quarter of the total. Each time a job became vacant, there was always an employee in the firm who recommended a close relation, a friend, or a relative, who was never of immigrant origin.[4]

However, it is imperative to go beyond the notion of institutional racism. It is really part of a way of thinking, undoubtedly influenced by the triumphant structuralism of the 1960s and 1970s, in which the structures or the system can be separated from the actors in the analysis. In the preceding example, the actors – the human resources department in the firm, the employees – seem at first sight to have nothing to do with the discrimination observed, which is said to be systemic. Wholly integrated into the structure, the discrimination appears to be related to procedures, disassociated from any prejudice and, further still, from any ideology. But the idea of institutional racism enables the exoneration of those who benefit symbolically from the discrimination or who at least are totally indifferent to the injustice which the victims suffer and who are apparently totally unaware and even innocent. In reality, it indicates that a veil of ignorance can conceal the reality of discrimination until the day when it is removed either because the victims establish the reality or, to pursue with our example, a team comprising trade unionists and sociologists decides to tackle the problem head-on. Once established, the racism in question can no longer be institutional, since the maintenance or the disappearance of discrimination now only depends on the action of the agents concerned, of their desire, or not, to become actors of change – which, we should point out, is what happened in the factory studied by Bataille and the CFDT. We should note in passing that we have here a particularly successful illustration of what we have called the *sociological commitment*:[5] the researcher, as a result of his or her intervention as a researcher, contributes to transforming a problem which has not been dealt with, and has not even been openly expressed, in a situation where there is apparently no provision for action, into a discussion and policy formulation. It reveals the existence of a form of racism which at the outset is institutional; once this is revealed, it becomes the priority issue for action within the system.

The era of 'cultural' racism

In the late 1970s and the beginning of the 1980s a second observation began to be made, once again first in the United States, then fairly early in Great Britain, and, thereafter, in France or in Belgium: racism was changing and cultural rather than physical characteristics were now being attributed to its victims. Thus in the United States, psychologists and political scientists developed the notion of *symbolic racism*. In this perspective black Americans were no longer accused of being intellectually inferior as a result of their physical differences, but of being incapable of adapting to the values of American society as a result of their cultural differences, which were said to be insurmountable. In the neo-liberal climate of the Reagan era, black Americans were described as refusing the American 'credo' and were said to prefer to live on social welfare rather than to work to better themselves socially; they were said to have no concept of family life.

At almost the same time, this form of racism was detected in Margaret Thatcher's Britain by Martin Barker, a political scientist, who spoke of *new racism* to describe the way in which recent immigrants were rejected because of their cultural characteristics, which were said to prevent them adapting to the values of the British nation – a nation which they were henceforth endangering. A little later in France, Étienne Balibar and Immanuel Wallerstein described a similar type of process and Pierre-André Taguieff spoke of *differentialist racism* when making a comparable observation. From this point on, the vocabulary became richer, *cultural racism* or *neo-racism* was discussed, and new debates developed. To what extent was there a break with the classical, scientific racism which focused on the physical or biological human 'races'? Had we entered a period in which racism would aim not so much to treat its victims as inferior, particularly at work, by over-exploiting them but rather to reject them, or even destroy them? Instead, should we not admit that at all times, racism combines dimensions of differentiation (and therefore of rejection or destruction) and dimensions of inferiorization?[6]

The fact remains that the period of the 1980s to 1990s is not only the time when the resurgence of racism is recorded in numerous societies but also the time when an interest is taken in its cultural aspects – even if the discussions are inconclusive. For if at this point, the cultural characteristics of the victims seem, for racism, insurmountable or not adaptable to the culture of the larger society, is this not because these characteristics refer back to the idea of a physical nature and attributes?

This cultural dimension of racism was pinpointed and analysed in a historical context in which the societies in question were subject to profound change. They were emerging with difficulty from the industrial age and discovering new, or recurrent, social difficulties: unemployment, exclusion, vulnerability, the urban crisis of the French *'banlieues'* or of the American 'hyperghettos' described by William J. Wilson,[7] the rise of what has sometimes been described as an *underclass*. At the same time, they were entering a phase of a massive upsurge of cultural identities. These were becoming socially more firmly entrenched, ethnicized, and fragmented and racism constituted the dark side of these processes, the reaction in a time of crisis of those who were anxious about their cultural existence, about their national identity, for example. And since specific cultural identities thrive and demand recognition to such an extent that at times they compete with one another, they also include radicalized dimensions in which racism can quickly find a hold.

Discrimination and racialization

In the 1980s–1990s, at the time when Europe was rediscovering racism, it was primarily perceived as an ideologico-political phenomenon, perhaps being capitalized on by the extreme-right forces which were then rising or re-emerging, such as the Vlaams Blok in Flanders, the Ligua del Norte in Italy, or the Front National in France. The other forms of the phenomenon – violence, prejudice, and discrimination – were not ignored, but the main struggle was political and fairly general. However, gradually, an idea was forging its way: to reduce racism it would not suffice to wage a frontal attack on the ideological and political level against the political forces which substantialize it. Racism in all its aspects had to be confronted head-on.

Confronting discrimination

Hence the theme of forms of discrimination came to the fore (this, moreover, was not restricted to racism and, for example, extended to sexism) and there was increasing concern to combat it on the ground in all spheres: employment, work, access to schooling, health, housing, leisure activities, the presence of 'visible' minorities on television, and so on. An increasing number of surveys zoomed in on this phenomenon, revealed it, gave details, while at the same time discussions were developing about the strategies to oppose it. For example, should 'positive discrimination' approaches be adopted? Can we implement legal measures if we do not have 'diversity statistics'? The novelty here was not so much the forms of discrimination as the central role which they began to occupy, visibly, in public life, to the extent that at times they seemed to take the place of racism. Thus, for example, in a highly successful book, *The End of Racism*, Dinesh D'Souza stated that in the United States, racial discrimination by white Americans towards black Americans was a rational form of behaviour which had very little connection with racist opinions: the shopkeeper who refused entry to his shop to a young black man, the taxi driver who did not stop to pick him up were, according to him, acting rationally and were not racist – their practice was not based on stereotypes or prejudice.[8]

Without going as far as supporting viewpoints as radical as this, this increase in importance of the theme of discrimination led to discussions which contrasted with those which concerned the ideologico-political dimensions of racism. It was not a question of a confrontation between anti-racism, on one hand, and political forces capitalizing on and using racism in their strategy, on the other, but, rather, a fairly wide consensus about the issue at stake – reducing discrimination – in parallel with controversies concerning political philosophy or culture, well beyond the traditional, partisan divisions.

While a relative consensus does exist as to the unacceptable nature of racial discrimination, this is also the result of a heightened awareness in our societies of the subjectivity of individuals. Admittedly, not everything is new, and in the past many important studies on racism bore witness to this awareness and more precisely to the keen consciousness of the personal experience of those targeted by racism – in many respects the work of Albert Memmi could illustrate this remark. It is nevertheless a fact that, from the 1980s, the research was reinvigorated by studies, particularly in Great Britain and the United States, focusing on the way in which the experience of racism has a long-lasting and traumatic effect on individuals, creating 'hidden injuries' and shaping subsequent forms of behaviour dominated by anxiety. An analysis can be found, for example, in the work of Joe Feagin and Melvin Sikes.[9] Ordinary forms of discrimination ('everyday racism'), each of which is apparently minor, have an effect on the moral and intellectual integrity of the individual, and go as far as affecting their personality.[10]

Thus, in the more specific sphere of racism and its study we find all of the following: the increasing openness of the social sciences to everything concerning the Subject; the increasingly widespread adoption of the victims' point of view, and not only that of the established order or of the state, when the issue is one of violence; the general interest taken in the Subject, who is crushed, denied, powerless, incapable of constructing him- or herself, and in the *Floating Subject* described in chapter 2 of this book. This means that we can no longer be satisfied with prioritizing the study of the production of racism or its sources; we must also take its effects into consideration – in return this should enable us to have a better understanding of its production.

One important consequence of this development, which sets forms of discrimination at the centre of the analysis of racism, as of the anti-racist struggle, is that we cannot avoid the discussion – which is crucial – about the recognition of ethnic or racial difference.

Getting to grips with diversity

To counter discrimination efficiently would the best thing not be to draw up a list, get to know the forms it takes, and evaluate them? This type of perspective rapidly leads to the idea that to do this it is essential to establish the existence of groups which are subject to discrimination and to estimate their numbers. This is one of the sources of the intensification of 'ethnicization' in present-day societies, and not only in Europe or in North America. All over the world, processes of ethnicization are associated with combating racial discrimination and conveyed by the groups concerned or by the intellectuals who adopt their point of view. We observe that with 'ethnicity' what was distant and exotic enters the very core of Western societies. Symmetrically, it is because groups of this type exist and are developing, and because cultural differences, to some extent naturalized, are becoming a central issue of collective life, that demands for the recognition of identities are on the increase. If need be, these include quantitative dimensions with figures and the establishment of statistics. A dialectic has been created resulting in the increasingly frequent use of the vocabulary of diversity, ethnicity, but also of race.

The phenomenon is valid in the first instance at the level of states, and it is at this level also that the discussions are the most intense. There is something disquieting about the link between the ethnicization of collective life and the struggle against discrimination; it is not restricted uniquely to being an expression of social progress. We would like to stress, for example, that 'diversity statistics' – to use the expression which has recently become fashionable, perhaps because it is more vague and consensual, and is less heavily connoted, than that of 'ethnic statistics' – can also be used to discredit a whole group. For example, counting the prison population of black people in the United States, or of Muslims in France, may lead to establishing a link between the figures for delinquency and crime and the sizes of these two groups, and, from then on, formulating policies for combating delinquency and crime specifically targeting them – and therefore stigmatizing them.

But the discussion also takes place at other levels. A particularly interesting case is that of diversity management (which in firms consists mainly of hiring personnel of various ethnic origins). Knowing whether this is a strategy which benefits only the management of companies, or serves to reduce racism and discrimination, is a question that is local – company level – national – for companies above a certain size – but also global – for multinationals.[11]

In countries with a culture open to multiculturalism and the recognition of minorities, and particularly in the Anglo-Saxon world, the very principle of giving them an official and quantified visibility, including in the national census, comes up against the difficulties inherent in the very nature of the problem: who decides on which group a person belongs to – the person themselves (auto-definition), the group and its leaders, or public authorities? A combination of these three possibilities? The criteria here are eminently problematic, for a definition which claims to be objective, based, for example, on physical attributes like skin colour, will clash with a subjective definition, based on the choice of the persons concerned, and vice versa.

The fact that a person can choose but also renounce an identity, and, more broadly speaking, the weight of the processes of production and invention of identities, results in the latter being permanently in evolution, fragmenting, decomposing and recomposing, which makes it difficult, if not almost impossible, to fix a stable image of a population with the components of its identity. Other categories have to be constantly introduced, for example, in each population census, which challenges the relevance of the very principle of categorization. This problem also goes for the categories closest to 'race'. Racialization is a dimension of the emergence of 'diversity' and it also gives rise to processes of fragmentation and recomposition. Thus in the United Kingdom as from the 1980s, minorities of Indian sub-continent origin demanded that an end be put to calling them 'black' – they wanted to differentiate themselves from minorities of African or Caribbean origin. One implication of these processes of cultural, racial, and social fragmentation is that numerous groups characterized each by an identity, a memory, a culture, an ethnic and religious belonging, and so on, find themselves possibly being at one and the same time both victims of and guilty of racism. Racism itself is being fragmented and increasing, targeting racialized individuals even when they have no obvious community of belonging; in return, through the mechanism of the self-fulfilling prophecy,[12] this may lead to the constitution of groups.

In countries where the political culture is strongly resistant to any recognition of differences in the public sphere, these questions are only posed once this resistance has already been breached. Until then, the problem is characterized by the firm opposition of the partisans of a form of universalism hostile to taking specificities into consideration and their denunciation of any vague project of multiculturalism, supporters of which are deemed at best naïve, and more likely traitors or, in the words of a journalist in the 1980s, 'rioters'.[13] Thus in France, in the name of the republican ideal, which only recognizes individuals who are free and equal before the law, it long appeared inconceivable that diversity statistics could be established – this non-recognition was in fact fraught with a certain hypocrisy because nobody had ever protested when, for example, demographic studies established the number of Jews in this country.[14] After the riots in October–November 2005, which clearly exposed the shortcomings of the 'republican model of integration', the question of the legacy of colonialism and its present-day extensions became central. A Black movement, the Representative Council of Black Associations (CRAN), appeared and a few months later one of the main tabloids (*Le Parisien*, 31 January 2007) published the findings of a survey showing the number of black people in France and the massive character of the discrimination to which they were subjected. Despite the controversies, and not only in connection with this survey, over the past few years the most convinced 'republicanist' positions have been considerably weakened: the French argument is changing and is moving closer to that of the Anglo-Saxon world. We should add here that the European Community is very active in this sphere, legislating, publishing comparative data, and exerting on member countries an influence in a direction which is more favourable to the Anglo-Saxon model than to the French-style republican universalism.

The theoretical and political tensions which are revealed or exacerbated by the growing sensitivity to discrimination oppose two conceptions of public space – universalist versus open to differences. Universalism itself can be presented in social terms. Are the forms of injustice and inequality through which discrimination is manifested not in the last resort social? These include access to employment, consumption, housing, education, health, presence in jobs in firms which involve responsibility or visibility, in the media, and so on. Consequently, to combat them would it not be better to avoid all ethnicization, forget cultural or ethno-racial differences, and only take into consideration categories which are social in the strict sense, defined in terms of income, for example? Do the racialized groups not themselves have an interest in investing in 'class' associations, as do the Afro-Brazilians studied by Livio Sansone,[15] presenting themselves from the point of view of being dominated or socially excluded, rather than focusing on an identity of race or of colour or even of culture? Would black people not gain by stressing their 'blackness' without presenting themselves from the viewpoint of ethnicity, focusing on the colour of their skin, to expose the injustice and social discrimination from which they suffer?

On another level, as compared with the 1980s and 1990s, when political philosophy and the social sciences focused primarily on accounting for the newness of 'cultural' or 'differentialist' racism, present-day discussion is changing. Today, it is increasingly clear that behind the concept of culture, that of nature is making a dramatic return; the obsessive fear of threat to one's cultural existence, in particular to one's nation, is conveyed by processes of fear and rejection in which physical race, biological or genetic attributes, beginning with the colour of the skin, have considerable weight. Old forms of racism in which ideological and pseudo-scientific theorizations explained the qualities and the failings of individuals by their belonging to hierarchically ranked human races have considerably declined. On the other hand, they return at lightning speed, or at least they survive, as soon as one considers forms of racial discrimination which are one of their main manifestations in today's democracies.

Classical racism operated quite openly and was incorporated at the highest level of ideologies and political action, including that of the state, as in South Africa. At the present time, racism is more diffuse, 'veiled', less explicit, but it nonetheless conserves a content of references to physical characteristics of the groups and the individuals targeted. The refusal on racist grounds of employment, accommodation, and so on, may include cultural aspects; it also includes a rejection based on the physical characteristics of the victims.

The paradox of the anti-discrimination struggle is that while it does constitute progress, materially mobilizing public authorities as well as associations, NGOs, companies, major organizations, intellectuals, and journalists, at the same time, by exacerbating, or at least by revealing, the tendency of societies to ethnicization and racialization, it contributes thereto. These tendencies are themselves a source of considerable ambivalence. On one hand, they enable actors to constitute themselves collectively and to act, including in the anti-racist struggle. But, on the other, they contribute to cultural, social, even racial fragmentation, endangering social ties, complicating the integration of each individual, and encouraging certain minorities to withdraw into communitarian forms of behaviour, with all the dangers that this implies. These include the subordination of individuals to the law of the group and its leaders, intercommunity tensions, and the refusal of universal values in the name of traditions or of religion.

The role of the social sciences here is certainly not to come to an over-hasty conclusion – for or against racialization or ethnicization. In the first instance, it is to analyse these tendencies, in all their contradictions and their implications. From the point of view of the state, for example, fighting for socio-economic equality is one thing, combating racial prejudice is another. From the point of view of a militant organization, the refusal of racism is one thing, asserting oneself as a racial or ethnic actor is another. From the point of view of the Subject, constituting oneself as an individual to endeavour to enjoy the same rights as any other individual is one thing, endeavouring to be recognized as being part of a specific collective identity is another. In this last instance, presenting oneself uniquely as a victim (for example of past, colonial racism, or the slave trade, or of present-day racism) is one thing, putting forward a positive, cultural, even racial identity, as was the case for 'negritude',[16] is another. The basic elements of the problem are many and somewhat varied, contradictory, or ambiguous. The most sophisticated answers and, in the long run, the most satisfactory are those which attempt to reconcile a maximum of these elements and to integrate as far as possible what seems to be incoherent or ambivalent; the most dramatic answers, on the contrary, are those which strengthen one single element, but this leads to ideological confrontations which at times are violent and not very productive.

Global racism

As the 1980s and 1990s approached, racism was being considered in the framework constituted by national societies or nation-states. In the United States they talked of *symbolic racism*, in Britain of *new racism*, and in France of *differentialist racism*. But we can no longer analyse racism by confining our thinking within the bounds of nation-states alone. The phenomenon tends to be increasingly global and the outcome of the dual time–space compression evoked in David Harvey's phrase (see chapter 5, p. 114). In ways which vary from one concrete experience to another, racism combines planetary – in any event supranational or transnational – dimensions, and others referring to local, national specificities or references; similarly it aggregates present-day aspects – mechanisms for discrimination, for instance – with historical dimensions, for example the impact of slavery, or colonization.

Here, anti-Semitism can serve as a paradigm. It has always been transnational, if we can be permitted this anachronism, located at planet level. From Antiquity, if we read the work of Peter Schäfer,[17] anti-Judaism (the term 'anti-Semitism' was only used from the 1880s) operated on three distinct sites: Egypt, Syria-Palestine, and Rome. Thereafter it was widely 'globalized' by Christianity, which at an early date conferred on it its world-level dimensions. But what present-day globalization provides is no less specific to the contemporary world. For today anti-Semitism cannot be analysed seriously without constantly bearing in mind the articulation of what is happening within the framework of the nation-states concerned, beginning with the countries with a Jewish population (mainly Israel, the United States, and some European countries, in the first place France), with the aspects which extend beyond or are not contained within this framework; without combining consideration of local elements and transnational elements, starting with those which have an impact on issues concerning the Near or Middle East. Nor can anti-Semitism be analysed without understanding how it implements elements borrowed from various repertories: the accusation of ritual crime of old-style Christian anti-Judaism; *The Protocols of the Elders of Zion*, forged for the rulers in the Kremlin at the end of the nineteenth century; Nazism; and so on.

The same thing is true if other forms of racism are considered. The recent French experience which we will consider in the first instance from the angle of anti-Arab and anti-Muslim racism is a good illustration of this statement. Today France has an immigrant-origin population from the Arab-Muslim world which is estimated, not strictly reliably to be sure, at approximately 5 million people, or about 7 to 8 per cent of the total population. And the racism which affects this population is an established phenomenon, whether it be a question of opinions and stereotypes or yet again, and predominantly, all sorts of discrimination in employment, access to housing, and in particular to certain forms of leisure. Sociological research also demonstrates that this population is the victim of segregation rampant in state schools. There is a form of 'educational apartheid'[18] which produces and reinforces inequalities for children of immigrant origin, instead of diminishing them, which is the aim of the republican ideal, or at least merely reproducing them, as the sociology of the 1960s and 1970s suggested.

But this racism does not only develop according to the tensions and crises specific to French society. It owes a lot to external processes and balances of power decided at a level which is quite different from that of the nation-state. Thus, several affairs or episodes demonstrate that the opinion of the outside world could have an impact on its evolution. In 1990, when France was preparing to participate in the first Gulf War and then became involved, the authorities took various measures to avoid the unrest which an involvement of this type could bring about within the population of Arab-Muslim immigrant origin. These measures were not in themselves racist, but they in fact exerted a racism which took several forms: stigmatization of this population suspected or accused of not being totally integrated or capable of being integrated; racist functioning of the police who stopped and searched young people on the basis of their facial features; a ban on certain trips (for example, secondary schools in the Parisian suburbs which have many children of immigrants were not allowed to organize visits to exhibitions or outings to the theatre in Paris during this period). The international policy of the country reinforced domestic racism. At the same time, the way in which the French media dealt with this conflict was perceived as particularly odious in some Arab-Muslim countries, which made their opinions known. French racism became a subject for international discussion and pressure while at the same time its development was over-determined by choices in international politics.

Another example: when France voted a law forbidding 'visible' signs of religion in state schools (March 2004), to prevent, in fact, the wearing of the Muslim 'headscarf', a few voices were raised to expose a vaguely racist political choice, for in reality it only targeted young Muslims – people spoke of Islamophobia. But above all much stronger criticisms came from abroad, either from Muslim societies, or yet again from the Anglo-Saxon world, criticizing the racist connotations of this law. Criticisms of this type sustained the French discussion, hardened some in their 'republicanism', their fixed conception of the republican idea in the name of which the law had been voted, and encouraged others to criticize it with the justification that it raised suspicions of racism.

In fact, everything connected with Islam is likely to 'globalize' racism and to make of it a problem which can no longer be considered strictly within the context of the nation-state alone. What is true for France is valid for other countries too. For example, the terrorist attacks in Madrid (March 2004) or in London (July 2005) had the effect of (but also partly caused) a foregrounding of the racism specific to Spanish or British society. Muslims in the two countries in question felt threatened by the reactions of national populations, who were more or less prepared to accuse all of them and even to suspect immigrants, in general, of being the cause of this terrorism. Similarly, the striking reactions throughout the Muslim world to the publications of caricatures depicting the Prophet Muhammad, in the first instance in a Danish daily newspaper, then in many others in Europe, denounced what they considered to be blasphemous contempt in these drawings, a contempt which was then often described as racist. In some countries, the protests took a violent turn, in others they were more moderate, particularly in Europe; in return they hardened the attitudes of some groups, including those on the extreme right, which found grounds therein for their racist hatred of the Arabs and Islam. Thus at the time in France the possibility of a swing in public opinion in favour of the Front National – a racist party – was evoked.

Nor is it possible to understand the racism specifically targeting black people if we restrict the analysis to the framework of nation-states. Today, the understanding of this phenomenon forces us to take into consideration on one hand supranational history which has led to segregation, stereotypes and the present forms of discrimination and, on the other, movements at world level and the present-day migrations of many black people. In some cases, the blacks are part of a diaspora – the 'Black Atlantic' for example, discussed by Paul Gilroy – characterized by their circulation between several countries. It may also happen – this is something of an understatement – that it is not easy for those who wish to migrate to accomplish this type of movement to leave an African country. The receiving or transit countries themselves operate immigration policies which are implemented with considerable violence as has been observed with Morocco and Spain, in Ceuta and Melilla, where the brutality used to control the frontier extends also into the desert where the Moroccan authorities drive back the migrants from sub-Saharan Africa in a manner which can be fatal. In this instance, the policy of countries in the North can be supported by courses of action implemented far away by

countries in the South and while they may not be intended
to be racist are nevertheless racially connoted.

In countries of residence, sometimes members of groups
who are themselves victims of anti-black racism reject the
newcomers who are also black precisely because of their
countries of origin. Thus, in the United States the descendants of slaves are not always tender with the new migrants
who come from sub-Saharan Africa or from the Caribbean,
and in France black Caribbeans are distinctly hostile to
migrants from sub-Saharan Africa. To a large extent, racism
targets migrant populations or the children of recent
migrants, with the result that problems of 'race' are confused
with those of immigration and contemporary migratory phenomena. From this point on, racism must be understood
globally because it brings into operation aspects linked to
the internal functioning of the societies concerned, and
others, associated with worldwide human, cultural, and economic currents; and, symmetrically, discussions about immigration are exacerbated by the issue of racism. As for many
other problems of society, it is often difficult to distinguish
clearly between the internal issues and the external ones, or
the inside and the outside; everything very rapidly becomes
intermingled.

This example of global anti-black racism can be extended
by taking into consideration an increasingly important issue:
the racist dimensions of the refusal to grant black Americans
the symbolic and material reparations which some of them
are demanding in compensation for the slave trade and
slavery. The refusal is a question which is both internal to
the United States (a country which in other respects has
championed the recognition of the Shoah and recognized the
wrongs done to the Japanese-Americans who were improp-
erly interned during the Second World War) and international because conveyed by American diplomacy, which is
endeavouring to oppose the reparations movement, which is
itself global. Pressure from numerous NGOs and states
which were formerly colonized support the demands of this

movement. This movement has been constituted on the basis of an ideology which is often 'pan-Africanist', diasporic – and therefore 'global'. Whether it be a question of the past, which concerns Africa, Europe, and the United States, or the present, anti-black racism can no longer be considered using the categories of the nation-state alone, nor can the identity and the action of those confronting it.[19]

Globalization has therefore transformed the spatial framework of the analysis of racism. Instead of saying that the phenomenon comprises national dimensions with, possibly, in addition international dimensions, we now have to approach it by endeavouring to understand it as being, increasingly, the end-product of complex interplay where internal processes and external, supranational processes constantly interact, combining and displacing each other.

Does another observation, of the same type but relative to anti-racism, not logically follow on, as has already been suggested by the Pan-African movement we mentioned? This is the idea of a link between 'global power', the hegemonic forces of the neo-liberal economy, and the way in which anti-racist ideas and practices have been circulating since the 1990s. This usually calls into question not globalization as such but the decisive role that the United States occupies therein, and it then constitutes a manifestation of the classical theses on American imperialism: in this perspective, the Americanization of the world is said to be shaping anti-racist action by imposing on it American categories of thought, whether it be a question of defining race, of advancing conceptions of the diversity of humankind, or of proposing policies, for example through the intervention of institutions like the World Bank or the IMF. It is said to lead to a racialization of the world. A radical and polemical variant of this viewpoint was proposed by Pierre Bourdieu and Loïc Wacquant, giving rise to keen reactions.[20] This approach reduced American influence to a process of imposition of categories which were themselves part of an imperialist rationale with no consideration of the elements of variety and criticism which characterize the discussion within the United States. It underestimates the internal dimensions of anti-racism, specific to national societies and the regions of the world where it occurs; it is said to give a distorted image of the intellectual exchanges between the United States and other countries, and so on. It is true that the present tendencies to ethnicization and racialization in many societies tend to narrow rather than to widen the gap between them and the United States. But from there to seeing therein the outcome of American imperialism there is a gigantic step which it would be ideological to take without specific studies. It seems to us to be preferable in this respect, as in others, to maintain the project of thinking 'globally' and therefore of analysing anti-racist action by following both paths: that of the influence of supranational and external forces – which cannot be reduced to the image of the hegemony of the United States – and that of the work of societies on themselves.

Racism and history

In his well-known study on race and history commissioned by UNESCO and published in 1952, Claude Lévi-Strauss observed that humankind had entered a phase of global civilization and that to do justice to the diversity of the various cultures which it comprises, it must be recognized that the relation which each has to time is itself variable.[21] But he did say that all societies are located in history. Now, for the past half-century a phenomenon of reversal has been taking place with respect to this image and there is a growing tendency for history to be in present-day societies. Over and above the distinction of the '*régimes d'historicité*' suggested by François Hartog[22] to indicate the different ways which societies have of thinking about time, it is the very place of historicity which is in question.

History becomes an issue; it appears as a resource mobilized in particular by all sorts of groups asking to be recognized in virtue of the dramas of which their ancestors were, or were said to have been, victims. As a result, racism is also loaded with historical themes; it is backed up by its own conceptions of the past, conceptions which some groups may possibly challenge. It rapidly acquires a wide-ranging historical input in which there is a mix of major omissions, on one hand, and suggestions which distort the past, on the other.

We have to evaluate this novelty. In the past the forms of racism which were based on biology or the physical aspects of the groups and individuals targeted had little resort to history. But today, memories are overlapping, competing with one another, and for both racism and anti-racism history is becoming essential. Here again, French experience can help us to illustrate this observation.

In France, anti-Semitism, as it was manifested particularly at the end of the 1990s, mobilized history constantly, as did the campaign against anti-Semitism. In the first instance, the movement crystallized around the Second World War and the role of the Vichy regime. In the 1980s, Jean-Marie Le Pen, the leader of the Front National, indicated his interest in the 'negationist' ideas of Faurisson, and on several occasions his anti-Semitism included remarks relative to this period. The existence of the State of Israel and everything associated with the Israeli–Palestine conflict have become another source, or another pretext for hating the Jews, and there again history is constantly mobilized or present – a history which is no longer that of France and which is focused on the Middle East – particularly if it is a question of drifting from legitimate support for the Palestinian cause towards attitudes with a distinct anti-Semitic connotation.

More recently, colonization, the slave trade, and slavery have become part of public discussion, in challenges to the national narrative from which they had been erased. Indeed, certain aspects have even been praised, so much so that in France in February 2005 a law was voted which included a clause (later deleted) requesting that the positive role of colonization be taught in history classes. Black movements in particular, but also political actors and committed intellectuals, have mobilized in the name of historical truth to refuse the silence or the minimization of the dramas experienced as a result of colonization or slavery; but also because they see therein, and quite correctly, a denial which is one of the sources of present-day racism, and which goes hand in hand with forms of discrimination at work now. To describe the colonial past as having made a positive contribution to colonized peoples is not only to call into question the intolerable nature of this same past. It is also in a way to perpetuate it or to revive it through prejudice, disregard, discrimination, and segregation. Racism does not always and everywhere combine the past and the present; it does not necessarily call upon both history and sociology. But each time this occurs it is intensified by this combination, which exacerbates it.

The dominant groups do not have exclusive rights to racism; it is even frequently sufficiently attractive in the eyes of the poorest to be instrumentalized by dictatorial, fascist, or totalitarian regimes, by demagogues or extremist parties with a strong working-class foothold. With cultural and social fragmentation and its ethno-racial expressions, it sometimes uses snatches of history, materials borrowed from the past, to develop between the bits and pieces. Thus there are still traces of anti-Semitism in France and, again, in the United States amongst black people, just as symmetrically Jews may manifest anti-Arab or even anti-black racism, and these traces can be sustained by discourse with historical pretensions. A ridiculous example is provided by the 'comedian' Dieudonné, ranting against what he claims to be the role of the Jews in the slave trade and, further still, leading us to believe that, on top of that, they wish to preserve the monopoly of historical suffering with the Shoah, consequently constituting a particularly potent obstacle to any recognition of the past tragedies which the slave trade and slavery were for black people.

The social sciences have not always countered racism vigorously, and in the past have even provided their own contribution to the production and diffusion of racist ideologies. One only has to look through the first issues of the major American sociological journal *The American Journal of Sociology* to realize this. For example, we find there articles by Francis Galton, or again a translation of the introduction to *The Aryan* by Vacher de Lapouge, one of the fathers of classical racism.

In the refashioned version of the phenomenon of racism, the sociological commitment[23] finds a particularly favourable and important terrain and can make a specific contribution to the anti-racist struggle. We list below the main points concerned.

Does racism mobilize the past? If so, history and historians should be in the front line to provide an impetus for changes in historical matters and not simply have them imposed from without, to ensure that the victims and the conquered are part of the historical narrative, and to provoke and shed light on public discussions. The rise and prospering of 'negationism' in France at the end of the 1970s was possible partly due to the lack of historical research on the Nazi death camps – it was not until the major colloquium organized by Raymond Aron and François Furet in 1982 that this gap was filled.[24]

If racism is becoming global, then anti-racism must also articulate global perspectives with references to local or national struggles at the same time, just as alter-globalization does in its best versions. Instead of controversies which rapidly become polemical and ideological, the social sciences can shed decisive light here by comparing experiences, examining their successes, failures, and difficulties, and by considering anti-racism, a little as we do social movements, both as an object for study and as an action whose capacity to rise to a high level of project involves the co-production of knowledge by researchers and actors.

Racism is not only an ideologico-political phenomenon; it is also conveyed in material ways, in particular in forms of discrimination. The social sciences must promote knowledge of these various forms and contribute to the discussions about the various sorts of knowledge which they call on. For example, the problem for the social sciences is not to make snap judgements as to whether or not one should be 'for' or 'against' statistics on diversity, but to construct the space for the discussion which these statistics evoke, to demonstrate their possible contribution but also their limits or even their possible dangers. It is then up to the actors, the leading associations and political parties, civil servants, and so on, to assume their responsibilities.

Racism is all the more pernicious today since victims sometimes tend to take refuge in the identities which communitarianism or relativism provides. The social sciences, after roughly forty years of discussion between universalists and relativists, 'Liberals' and 'Communitarians', 'Republicans' and 'Democrats', have nothing to lose by encouraging social, cultural, and political actors, public opinion and the media to endeavour to go beyond these cleavages and invent forms which combine the two types of values. Racism is sustained as much by withdrawal into identity as by proposing an over-abstract form of universalism – it originates in these two dangers. Ensuring its decline undoubtedly involves efforts being made in various places to refuse the imposition of a choice between universal values or recognition of differences and, on the contrary, learning to reconcile them.

Finally, racism can be manifested as an 'institutional' phenomenon. In these instances, the role of the social sciences is to expose what the institutions conceal and to reveal possible actors behind the structures and get them to confront their responsibilities. It is therefore also the task of the social sciences to indicate the concrete actions likely to modify the working of the organizations in a direction which will promote the reduction of racism. This calls for the deliberate intervention of actors within these organizations, or outside them, and favourable circumstances: for example, taking advantage of changes in the legislation.

There is no lack of paths for the social sciences to follow if researchers wish to contribute to reducing racism. Their task is not to give advice, setting themselves up as experts, or complacently exposing something – American imperialism or French republicanism, for example. Their task is to produce knowledge along with the actors concerned and to allow them to speak in their own words – not to take their place.

5

The New Arena of the Social Sciences, or: How to Raise the Level of Generalization

In the face of evil, violence, racism, or terrorism, it is now possible to propose new or updated modes of approach.

These methods of approach do not delineate a specific sphere, separate from the types of analysis which are emerging to deal with other social, cultural, or political problems. On the contrary, they are part of the framework of the reconstruction of a much broader theoretical arena within which the examination of a specific and restricted question – such as racism – can be articulated with other empirical concerns.

Two opposite poles stake out this new arena, enabling us to move from specific studies to general considerations. At one extreme we have the concept of the Subject, which we shall examine in depth in tackling evil, whereas habitually the concept of the Subject is used to envisage good. The other extreme, which acts as a reference in any endeavour to raise the level of generalization, refers to our capacity to think 'globally'.

Critique of the Subject

The concept of Subject is not new, and in intellectual life it is ever-present with its ups and downs. In some periods of history this concept predominates, in others it is concealed or misused, even hounded out. Thus in the post-war years Jean-Paul Sartre very successfully personified a philosophy of freedom and responsibility which clearly sets his work on the side of the Subject. For him, '[M]an is characterized above all by his going beyond a situation, and by what he succeeds in making of what has been made of him – even if he never recognizes himself in his objectification.'[1] In the 1960s the rise of structuralism marked the beginning of a phase of decline of the influence of the Subject, to the benefit of approaches which left little room for the subjectivity of actors. This was the time of Claude Lévi-Strauss, whose collected essays were published in *Structural Anthropology* in 1959, Jacques Lacan, Roland Barthes, Noam Chomsky, Michel Foucault, and many others who in one way or another then proclaimed the 'death of Man' – and therefore of the Subject.

This period is behind us. Inaugurated in the 1980s, the return of the Subject is today beyond doubt. Perhaps this is merely a question of a swing of the pendulum of the type recalled by Albert Hirschman in a classical book where he explains that societies periodically undergo movements on a grand scale, going from private interest to public action,[2] and vice versa. This would mean that we are in a global, historical phase favouring individualism. The fact remains that for the last twenty years we have been observing the widespread return of the Subject in the social sciences. This phenomenon is so spectacular that we need to assess it critically and take a hard look at the contribution of the concept of Subject, but also the limits or the problems which we may come up against if we use it. This is not the time to fight the enemies of the Subject – they have been defeated, in any event for the time being. Now we have to enrich the concept by discussing it.

The place of the Subject

For the time being at least, let us accept the definition proposed by Alain Touraine, this sociologist who successfully resisted and maintained the point of view of the Subject when confronted with the triumph of structuralism in the 1960s and 1970s and who, since the 1980s, more than anybody else, personifies its return today: 'I use the term *subject* to describe the construction of the individual (or group) as actor, through his efforts to transform events and experiences into a life-project. The subject is an attempt to transform a lived situation into free action.'[3]

The Subject thus defined, and therefore the subjectivity of the actors, has become essential in the social sciences today. Here are some illustrations.

Researchers who study religious phenomena observe that actors explain their faith as a highly subjective, personal decision. For example, many young people in the French *banlieues* say, 'If I'm a Muslim, it's by choice' and not something 'inherited', the mere reproduction of the religions of their parents and forebears. More generally speaking, and this is not a paradox, cultural and religious identities today are to a very large extent due to the personal subjectivity of those who claim to belong to them: they are produced rather than reproduced. They are the collective expression of individual choices which they aggregate; to return to a classical vocabulary, they are the outcome of personal *achievement*, self-fulfilment, much more than *ascription* – that is, the assignation to a pre-determined identity. This observation has also been made by sociologists as well as by social anthropologists or historians. Thus in the 1980s an important book edited by Eric Hobsbawm and Terence Ranger discussed the 'invention of tradition'.[4]

Researchers who are interested in the body and in the relationship to the body, to sport, dance, music and movement, tattooing, plastic surgery, and so on, observe that it is no longer possible, as it was in the past, to dissociate body and mind or nature and soul. The body belongs to 'the individual', and everything which affects it, changes it, and enhances it, even if it means suffering, is part of subjectivity. The work of David Le Breton is a good demonstration of how, in various domains, transcendence becomes self-transcendence; exceeding one's capacities may imply risking one's life. There is a change of direction in our social life, and in our analyses, which involves the enhancement and understanding of everything which links, and no longer separates, the work of the mind and the work on the body and everything that aims towards the exploration of oneself and one's own limits. Thus – the example is taken from David Le Breton – the figure of the adventurer is no longer the traditional one of the explorer of the world and its unknown areas, perhaps impelled on by a political or a scientific passion. It has become that of the apparently ordinary individual who takes part in an extreme experience in which his or her endurance, willpower, and courage are tested. The 'new adventurer' is the man or woman who rows across an ocean alone, tests his or her body, soul, and physical and moral capacities simultaneously.[5] And while the body can be thought of in the words of Anastasia Meidani as 'the locus of the self which acts', it also becomes 'a business deal and a commodity' – which invites us in our thinking to associate it with the theme of economic globalization: the body is at one and the same time held in the grip of this economic globalization and also in that of a subjective experience; it is a physical activity merged with issues of money, the media, advertising and economic knowledge, and a terrain for subjectivization, for the work of the Subject. This work does not necessarily lead to the improvement of the body; on the contrary, it may look more like a crisis, even self-destruction, and, for example, lead to obesity or anorexia.

Research which focuses on health and illness now devotes considerable space to the patient and his or her suffering – both physical and moral – and refuses to separate the patient from the illness. Thus Philippe Bataille's research gives us a new insight into the social and cultural approach to death by showing the extent of the importance assumed by the endeavours which are gradually taking shape in contemporary societies, particularly in hospitals, to reinforce the bonds between the dying, their loved ones, and their medical or community environment.[6] Research is increasingly alive to the theme of ethics and, for example, to decisions regarding life or death in situations where the person concerned is incapable of making his or her own choices known, or yet again regarding the major social choices such as those associated with adoption or medically assisted procreation. What, for example, is the view of Jean-Claude Ameisen, a biologist who is president of the Ethics Committee at the French National Institute of Health and Medical Research (INSERM)? He says that 'ethics in its constant recompositions aims to reinvent and preserve the concept of the Subject as the actor of his own life'. The approach to mental suffering, depression, stress, or to the 'weariness of the self', as Alain Ehrenberg[7] puts it, also forces us to take the reference to the Subject into consideration.

This acknowledgement of the Subject as an analytical tool can be extended to yet other domains. New light is shed on the study of the family, a classical field in sociology, by putting into perspective the personal Subjects found therein, forming, for example, what François de Singly[8] calls the 'democratic' family. The child, in contemporary social science, is no longer an immature being, a person in the making, who will become a fully adult individual in the course of a process of 'primary' socialization (in the family and at school), then 'secondary' socialization (at work, in community organizations, etc.); children are increasingly actors in their own right, capable of conferring a meaning on their acts – Subjects.[9] The sociology of education studies the pupil or the teachers as Subjects of their experience.[10] The sociology of racism found one of its most promising fields of research by studying how victims of racism are repudiated, denied as the Subject of their existence, and despised as human beings.

Feminist studies, still so deeply steeped in structuralist thought and, in the United States, by what is referred to as 'French Theory', have been gripped, in the words of the title of an important book by Judith Butler, by 'gender trouble', which refers to the efforts of actors, both men and women, to subvert identities and rid themselves of normative determinism and assignations which model gender. Brought up on the key structuralist authors, Butler does partly succeed in extricating herself to think in terms of ' "women" as the subject of feminism'.[11]

Work is another field where the Subject becomes an essential analytical tool, and the theme deserves to be developed to some extent. For Marx, in this instance the direct heir of Hegel, work is humans' creative activity par excellence and even their essence, a tremendous force for liberation, of progress for humankind and of self-fulfilment for individuals – but individuals are exploited and alienated as a result of the private ownership of the means of production. For Marx, and many others, the vocation of political action is precisely to ensure that work is not a form of alienation and to end the exploitation of workers. The sociology of labour, throughout the industrial era, focused on the relationship of domination in employment, on the modes of its organization, and on the strategic and class interaction of the actors which resulted from it; it constantly criticized Taylorism and other so-called 'scientific' forms of organization which led to 'piecemeal' work, to use Georges Friedmann's telling description.[12]

But, from the mid-1970s, new approaches focused on the changes affecting employment: it was said to have become more human, organized in a participatory manner, enabling all workers henceforth to have an overall view of their work. Autonomy was said to have taken the place of alienation, the division of labour no longer existed, and everyone could find self-fulfilment in work – a thesis which is questionable,[13] but which does have the merit, once again, of focusing on the Subject – here, a Subject socially defined as a worker. In this post-Taylorian context, some have even spoken of the end of work, or at least pleaded for an end to considering work as central to society and to seeing therein something essential to humanity or, at least, to social ties. For example, Dominique Méda questions whether the time has not come to 'disenchant work', and to put an end to the spell which this concept, laden with all sorts of hopes, utopias, and expectations, exerts on us and to 'ask by what other means we could enable individuals to have access to sociability, utility, integration, all things which work was able to and could still provide, but certainly not any longer in an exclusive manner'.[14]

The social sciences have obviously not abandoned the critical reflexivity which of necessity characterizes them. In the context created by the transformations of globalized capitalism, they have increasingly emphasized the way in which the very integrity of the individual, beyond work, but in instances where it is practised, may be affected. This is, I think, the meaning of the criticism which Richard Sennett makes of flexible capitalism,[15] in which employees are subjected not so much to the visible power of those in charge of the organization of labour, as they were when Taylorism was at its zenith, nor to that of the managers, as was thought in the 1970s or the 1980s, but to that of the shareholders, who constitute a distant and impersonal world. Indeed, today, the corporation, particularly when it has reached a certain size, may become a stressful and unstable world within which confidence is not the norm, where there is nothing to boost employees' self-esteem, and in which they are 'disposable' – a Kleenex which one throws away without a thought: the person who hires you may themselves have already been fired by the person who dismissed you and who will, shortly, be fired in their turn. In these circumstances, personal suffering at work, stress, harassment, whether sexual[16] or otherwise, in short everything associated with social or interpersonal relationships which ultimately results in calling into question the person concerned as a Subject, becomes extremely important. Modern individualism, by its entry into the world of work, leaves the weakest or the most vulnerable exposed to difficulties which make of them victims, individuals who become depressed or overcome by shame and who sometimes commit suicide or self-destruct. Negated in their very being, these individuals are no longer defined by their contribution to the corporation, nor even by the injustice which they feel when they compare their contribution with their salary; these persons are not so much robbed of the fruits of their labour as affected in the depths of their being: as Subjects.

Thus there have been considerable transformations in employment over time and the 1980s and 1990s saw the rise of what were on the whole rather gloomy predictions about its place in society or the condition of the workers – a term which is itself somewhat outdated, perhaps as a result of its being overused in Marxist or communist discourse, today on the wane. In this context, the introduction of the theme of the Subject has been implemented through the darkest of images or viewpoints, from the angle of the ill-effects of employment and the negation of the integrity of the human being. But this is only one side of the coin, and perhaps there is an even greater need to relativize it than might be thought. Thus Michel Lallement, at the end of an in-depth clarification, observes that 'work has not been dissipated in the mists of any sort of post-modernity or in the waters of increasingly "liquid" societies. It is still high on the axiological scale of European countries.'[17] Backed up by statistics, Lallement demonstrates that work 'is, today, increasingly, an imperative as a way of asserting oneself', and is strongly associated with happiness – he quotes, for example, a questionnaire survey carried out by Christian Baudelot and Michel Gollac. To the first question: 'What is the most important thing for you to be happy?' 27 per cent of those questioned answered spontaneously it was work![18] Introducing the perspective of the Subject in the analysis of work cannot therefore be restricted to including the alienation and destruction of individuals. It must also imply consideration of the self-fulfilment and creative dimensions which it conveys, or can convey, and therefore not lose sight of the approaches initiated by Hegel or by Marx.

From religion to employment, as we see in these illustrations, on all sides the social sciences devote considerable space to the Subject, which has become a central category in many analyses. True, the Subject had never completely disappeared from social thinking, even at the height of structuralism in the 1960s and 1970s. Important currents of

research in the social sciences have always kept this traditional inspiration alive, including in France, undoubtedly the
country in which structuralism had the largest arena in the
world. Resistance, implicit rather than theorized, was to be
found in the work of Alain Touraine, as we have said, but
also of Edgar Morin, Claude Lefort, Georges Balandier, and
Henri Lefebvre in so-called 'clinical sociology', or, yet again
in the 1970s, with the rise of methods focusing on listening
and taking an interest in 'life histories' – a field in which the
Italian social sciences played a decisive role.[19]

From that point on, the Subject moved from the margins
to the centre; it is the core of many theoretical schemes and
of many concrete approaches. If such a spectacular development was able to take place in barely a few years, it is not
only the result of the movement of ideas, as if this was
autonomous, or, in any event, unconnected to the movement
of societies. It is also because the rise of personal subjectivity,
in all areas, is a decisive element in the overall rise of modern
individualism and this can be observed in all sectors of collective life – which, moreover, justifies us in talking about a
'second modernity', as does, for example, Ulrich Beck. It is
also because the classical approaches, in terms of integration
and socialization, which take the idea of society as their
point of departure, seem increasingly inappropriate; so much
so that there is talk of discarding this idea, or even that of
the 'social' – an extreme point of view which is shared by
sociologists as different as Alain Touraine and Bruno Latour,
for example.[20]

The return of the Subject

Today, on the whole it has become difficult to reject the
concept of the Subject by accusing it purely and simply of
constituting a metaphysical illusion. Yet this was the basis
used by structuralist thought to oppose the idea that humans
could be aware of and responsible for their acts.

Throughout the 1960s and 1970s, this structuralist
thought made the Subject into an enemy, which it hounded

and pursued, whose death it wished to announce, claiming to reveal structural causalities or, in the words of the philosopher Louis Althusser and the Althusserian Marxists, over-determinations 'of last resort'. The idea of conflict between actors was replaced by that of objective contradictions, often dreaming also of crisis and revolutionary convulsions, leading, in some extreme cases, to a call to armed struggle and involvement in the spiral of terrorism. For the leading thinkers inspired by structuralism, the functioning and evolution of societies are dominated by the weight of authorities, structures, systems, abstract mechanisms, and to admit the idea of Subject is a mistake or a naïvety: we are nothing but a plaything of forces which escape us. One had to establish rules, systems, and codes, along the lines of Saussurian linguistics, and certainly not reveal and understand actors. In the most radical variants of structuralism, it was a question of 'process without subject'. Louis Althusser lent Marxist credibility to anti-humanism, and Pierre Bourdieu advanced a concept which enabled him to eliminate the Subject: from his point of view, individuals are unconsciously determined in their perceptions, their thoughts, and their behaviour by an attitude inculcated during their socialization, what he calls *habitus*.[21]

Structuralist thought has not entirely disappeared; today it still nurtures political movements or tendencies dominated by rationales of suspicion and postures of pure denunciation. It is the driving force, more or less explicitly, of hypercritical leftism, which speaks uniquely in terms of all or nothing, which demands absolute change as opposed to any project for democratic change obtained through gradual reform, negotiation, and the interaction of social or political actors. At times we still find the trace in important books or articles. Thus one of Pierre Bourdieu's last books, *Masculine Domination (La domination masculine)*, still in many respects comes under this form of structuralism which is so alien to the concept of Subject; if we are to believe him, women are dominated by men to such an extent that they can only internalize the very categories in which men conceive this domination. They are reduced to the state of victim, which makes it impossible for them to constitute themselves as Subjects. A symbolic form of violence is said to prevent the Subject from constructing itself as such. When this book came out, militant feminists criticized this conception sharply, stressing, on the contrary, that women did have a conscience and a capacity to act, a theme which is at the centre of a recent survey by Alain Touraine which resounds like a reply to Bourdieu.[22] It is precisely because there are actors that structuralist thinking seems at times so visibly out of step with observable reality.

There are now hardly any partisans as intransigent as yesterday in the camp of those opposed to any notion of Subject, perhaps also because on their side those who defend the point of view of the Subject have introduced some nuances. This is explained by Vincent Descombes:

> The cut-and-dried positions of yesterday are no longer in vogue. On one hand, the opponents of the subject accept to make room in philosophy for a Subject, on condition that it is a little closer to what human experience reveals: on condition that this subject which I am supposed to be is divided, fragmented, often unclear to itself and sometimes powerless, as I am myself. On the other hand, those in favour of the subject assert that it is not possible to consider the idea of the subject to be an illusion, but concede that it has never existed except in a divided, fragmented, unclear and powerless mode. In short, everyone seems disposed to say that the subject had been conceived, erroneously, as if possessing two attributes to which it was not entitled: *transparency* and *sovereignty*.[23]

Thus, according to Descombes, today the *'metaphysical'* subject would be relinquished and replaced by a 'post-metaphysical' subject.

The autonomy of the subject

The etymological meaning of subject – from the latin *subjectum* ('sub-mit') – is in contradiction with the meaning which it has acquired today. In its present meaning, the Subject is not the person who is subject to the authority of a sovereign – a very classical definition. We have moved from subjection to autonomy – a move which, obviously, would deserve to be studied. Nor is the Subject the person who is subjected to observation, as in the experimental psychology of the 1950s and 1960s. It is defined by its capacity for autonomy, as being the source of its own representations and its own actions, of which it is, in Alain Renaut's words, the basis and the author.[24] For present-day social sciences, the subject has two sides.

One is defensive. In this case the Subject is what resists the rationale of the systems, the sovereign, God, a community and its law, or what eludes them; still from this point of view, it is also the capacity of the human being to act for his or her survival, to save his or her skin. For example, the psychoanalyst Jean Bergeret[25] explains, if we wish to understand the conduct of rage and violence of the young people in French *banlieues*, we must realize that in the first instance it is above all an act of survival in the face of a society perceived as a threat to their very existence. Personal resistance, refusal, rejection of imposed roles, norms, constraints – the Subject, in Alain Touraine's vocabulary, is initially 'empty'; it is primarily a 'struggle for survival in the face of the tremendous pressure from the economy, consumerism, mass culture and communitarianism', and, as a result, it is vulnerable, always threatened with being crushed and tempted, in some cases by fatal or self-destructive forms of behaviour: suicide, alcoholism, drugs, personality disorders, and so on.

The other side of the Subject is constructive, or perhaps positive; it is the capacity of being an actor, of constructing one's experience, it is, in the words of the German sociologist Hans Joas, the 'creative aspect of man'.[26] The Subject is not an essence or a substance; it is, from this point of view, the capacity to become autonomous and to control one's own experience.

It is a question of autonomy and not of independence because there is no exteriority in relation to social life. This definition stresses the capacity of the Subject to participate in modern life by making choices, taking decisions, and being responsible for one's acts. It thus re-connects with the philosophy of Jean-Paul Sartre. It implies that each individual capable of constituting his- or herself as Subject and therefore of manifesting his or her own desire for individuation recognizes in all other individuals the same capacity, sees a Subject in all human beings, endowed, like him- or herself, with the capacity to engage in a process of individuation. In other words, the sociology of the Subject is not indifferent to general questions of living together, or of politics: the Subject sees itself as being defined by a relationship with the City which is a relationship to oneself, a considered relationship with oneself. From this point of view, being a Subject implies taking a position as a thinking citizen, being interested in the City at the same time as in oneself; by introducing a subjective, considered relation to oneself, one is necessarily introducing a similar relation to the City.

We therefore have to clearly state that the sociology of the Subject is not a sort of depoliticized, a-historical, a-social psychology. Ultimately, the viewpoint of the Subject implies thinking about the social, the individual in society, confronting institutions, and so on. One might say, in the same vein, that the sociology of the Subject is a humanist sociology. But here we have to introduce an empirical observation: the dominant tendency in contemporary societies is a much greater concern with personal autonomy than with responsibility or solidarity. The viewpoint of the Subject asserts itself by establishing itself in opposition to the viewpoint of the system, social functioning, integration, which allows for much easier reference to the sense of community. This is what sustains the concerns of those who see therein the imprint, above all, of individualism and egoism.

The concept of the Subject must be distinguished from that of the actor. The actor only appears if there is a move from the capacity for action to actual action. This leads to thinking about the conditions favourable, or otherwise, to this move, which, in certain cases, may prove to be problematic, difficult, or even impossible. The Subject is capable of being an actor, may become one, but not necessarily. We should add that the term 'actor' also deserves to be discussed – if only because the category encompasses a large variety of highly disparate figures: leaders and performers, party managers and grassroots militants, and so on. Action does not present the same degree of autonomy for all its participants.

Similarly, the Subject must be distinguished from the individual, a wider category which includes the Subject, but also the fact or the desire of participating in modern life, consuming, having access to money, work, education, to health as an individual, to security also, which is not the same thing as acting. Modern individualism includes the subjectivity of people but is not restricted to it. One might, moreover, question to what extent the concept of the Subject should be integrated or associated with that of the individual and to what extent it would be better to separate them.

Finally, the sociology of the Subject does not exclude an approach in terms of inter-subjectivity, but this is of another nature. When Jürgen Habermas, for example, invites us to consider a contentious discussion between individuals – which he refers to as communicational acting – inseparable from the democratic spirit, he is not offering us a theory of the Subject. But it is not very far off, because in a Habermas-type discussion there does come a point at which everyone makes intellectual choices, adopts the arguments which they come round to after making a choice, a deliberation which is also internal, personal, subjective, and not only collective.

Two conceptions of the Subject

The present success of the Subject should not conceal the theoretical difficulties inherent in its concept; this should in itself be spelt out. An effort at conceptual clarification is all the more necessary as one very rapidly observes, as soon as the possible approaches to the Subject are examined in detail, that the propositions available do not necessarily correspond to a homogeneous and coherent whole. One could say of the Subject what Max Weber said of individualism – namely that the 'expression individualism includes the most heterogeneous things imaginable'.[27]

A convenient point of departure may help us to formulate the problem. In the sociology of Alain Touraine, the Subject functions prior to the social. It is even, in the first instance, that which resists the social: 'To be able to say "I" becomes the main brake upon the hold of the social over the actor.'[28] But how is this Subject constructed, where does it come from, and what is its foundation? The social sciences have long been thinking about the conditions of the foundation of society or of the community, but much less thought has been devoted to the foundation of the personal Subject, except to say that it is a direct product of the social bond, of the totality of institutions or processes of socialization. If the subject is non-social, does that mean that it pre-exists and is created prior to any social or interpersonal relation? The Subject would then seem to be virtually present in each individual and is only transformed into concrete behaviour, into action, if certain conditions are fulfilled. In this case should the Subject be considered a 'thinking, permanent, and original' substance, which could take us back to Saint Augustine? A conception of this type is contrary to that of the Subject constructing and constituting itself through thought processes themselves linked to experiences or to ordeals, in the words of Danilo Martuccelli.[29]

The problem is not new and was stated, in particular, by George Herbert Mead, of whom Hans Joas says:

> Mead shared unqualifiedly the universalist orientation of the question Kant posed, but he finds his predecessor's answer to the question unsatisfactory. If the conditions of objective knowledge are to be found in the knowing subject prior to all experience, then they stand outside all communality and precede all development of the human subject. If the basis for the possibility of responsible action cannot be found in

reality, and if that possibility remains a pure postulate, then we are in danger of abandoning ourselves permanently to a self-deception.[30]

It is not easy to decide in favour of one or other of the two main notions which we have thus begun to differentiate, and which deserve to be clearly contrasted, even if, in theory, it is possible to endeavour to articulate them and to envisage their possible complementarity. The Subject, in social sciences as in philosophy, can indeed be defined either as a principle acting prior to any action or any social experience, or, which is not totally contradictory, but very different, as forming itself as the action or the experience takes place and disintegrating in the course of the processes of subjectivization and de-subjectivization – processes which may go to the extreme: on one hand, hyper-subjectivization, plethora, or overload of subjectivity; on the other hand, self-destruction, suicide, martyrdom.

Is the Subject a construction or a quasi-anthropological attribute of each individual? Is it linked to a praxis, to use an old vocabulary, or is it a virtuality specific to any human being? Does it found itself in practice, action, or experience, or is it a pre-existing given? If one sees therein a principle at work operating upstream of the social, a principle which is therefore natural, anthropological, and non-social, we risk losing sight of what many consider is the cornerstone of the social sciences and one of the first of Émile Durkheim's legacies: the assertion that the social should be explained by the social.

As one might suspect, the theoretical issue at stake is not a minor one; it is the entire Durkheimian edifice which is threatened or challenged by approaches which valorize the Subject.

This question leads to what Vincent Descombes calls a 'vicious circle':

> There seems to be a vicious circle in the very idea of an agent who *becomes* autonomous by learning rational practices

(speaking, calculating, measuring, classifying, etc.) and techniques for self-government. But if this apparent contradiction is true, this means that an agent cannot now be
autonomous except if he or she has always been so, which
would amount to admitting that we will not find autonomous agents in this world as it is now. ... It would therefore
seem that a training course in autonomy is logically impossible: only an agent who is already autonomous could become
autonomous. One could say that the philosophy of the
subject, by postulating an operation of auto-position on the
part of the individual who acts autonomously, acknowledges
the difficulty constituted by this threat of a vicious circle.[31]

Is there a way out of this vicious circle? Can we extricate
ourselves from this problem whereby that which is to be set
up has already been set up, otherwise it cannot be set up?

Must one already be a Subject in order to become a
Subject?

The question runs through all philosophical debate. 'To
become a subject, one must already be a subject but, in fact,
one can only be a subject after having constructed oneself
as a subject,' observes Vincent Descombes in his commen-
tary on Michel Foucault.[32] One way of finding a successful
way out of this problem might be to stop opposing the idea
of the Subject which pre-exists itself and the Subject which
constructs itself in experience; why not endeavour to articulate the two, making allowance for each? In this perspective,
there is an anthropological potentiality, a human quality –
the capacity of being a Subject – and this is, or is not, implemented in processes of subjectivization which are processes
of self-transformation for which the persons concerned are
themselves responsible. From this point of view, each is then
the actor, or the author, or the Subject of his or her own
subjectivization, which may nonetheless owe a lot to others,
to those who aid or guide in these processes, school teachers,
for example, who assume the task of changing people and
who know that they cannot do it without these same people.

When one is taught by someone else, one is the co-producer
of this education. One is not the passive receptacle; one is

transformed as the result of the intervention of another person, and because, at the same time, one performs work on oneself. This is the path explored by Cornelius Castoriadis, who speaks of human subjectivity as being 'reflective' and 'having the capacity for deliberate activity', and explains that 'autonomy [of the Subject] is created by the self-exertion of autonomy, which presupposes, in a certain manner, that it pre-exists itself'.[33] We can go one step further here and distinguish between two complementary rationales of subjectivization, depending on whether it is self-subjectivization or hetero-subjectivization, the intervention of other people, aid, or yet again imposition from without, possibly in the form of constraint. It may even be necessary to distinguish between numerous modes of subjectivization, an idea that we find in Michel Foucault:[34] some come under self-subjectivization and are the outcome of a renunciation, others come under trans-subjectivization, an effort to become oneself in some way.

This theme of renunciation is important as it enables us to evaluate in the case of the Subject what separates contemporary societies from traditional societies. If we follow the anthropology of Louis Dumont, it is by leaving social life that individuals, in 'holistic' Indian society, can become self-sufficient entities, Subjects, which he refers to, in the terminology of Max Weber, as 'renunciates' ('*sannyasin*').[35] The Subject here is constructed or asserts itself through a process of renunciation and disengagement and not in social life. In this sense, the Subject in traditional societies is very unusual since it finds the conditions for its existence in disengaging from social life and not in belonging to it. Now today, the opposite seems to be decisive: becoming a Subject, or even, much more generally, an individual, does not mean leaving social life but, on the contrary, participating fully in it, finding therein the conditions for self-fulfilment and an autonomy which does not mean exteriority. Modern individuals, in their dimensions as Subjects, are at the opposite extreme of the renunciate of Max Weber or Louis Dumont; the Subject is socialized and not de-socialized.

Modern subjectivization is socialization and not de-socialization – a very unusual form of socialization since it holds out against norms and the powers that be. But we have not yet decided here between the two principal propositions which have just been set out: the one which considers that the Subject pre-exists action and the one which considers that the Subject is constructed or destroyed in action. This is because we see therein two analytical tools which a practical approach could easily attempt to use as two different perspectives in tackling a concrete, historical experience. Vincent Descombes' 'vicious circle' must not be a source of paralysis, of incapacity to analyse; we can make of it a dual-purpose instrument which enables a better understanding of reality.

A dark side?

Could it be that our definition of the Subject which we have been working with up till now and the discussions which it raises are somewhat simplistic? The resulting concept, even if it is not stabilized and is visibly torn between the two processes which we have just differentiated, only focuses on its bright side, its capacity for legitimate or comprehensible defence and its creative capacity leading possibly to action. In our working definition we have until now focused on a principle of reciprocity: being a Subject implies that we acknowledge that any human being must also be able to be one. But should the concept not be enlarged and include what I have referred to, for lack of a better expression, as the anti-Subject, the dark side of the Subject, its destructive side, including in particular cruelty, violence for the sake of violence, and therefore the negation of others as Subject?[36]

Once again, for this discussion, we can begin with what Alain Touraine says when questioned about the hypothesis of a 'negative' dimension of the Subject, bearing in mind that he promotes a 'positive' image of the Subject. The question preoccupies Farhad Khosrokhavar, who constantly asks him: 'Why would the Subject not contain a dark side within itself?'[37] Might it be that this sociologist who has first-hand experience of the horrors of the Iranian revolution is fascinated by lethal rationales? This is what Touraine seems to think; when talking about racism, violence in the *banlieues*, and terrorism, he replies, 'You are attracted by "de-subjectivization." '[38] But resorting to the idea of de-subjectivization only enables us to cover part of the sphere of behaviour which implies the destruction and the negation of the subjectivity of others. It leaves aside the capacity to become the author of behaviour whose meaning derives directly from the pleasure of causing suffering or which seems to be bereft of meaning given the extent of passivity faced with others' suffering. There is not always and every-where a search for meaning, and when none is to be found, this cannot be reduced to a deficit, as Touraine thinks: 'I see no fundamental reason for saying that there is always neces-sarily meaning. On the other hand, when there is no meaning, there is awareness and suffering from the loss of meaning.'[39] But there can also be sadism, or gratuitous violence, pleasure in humiliating or destroying, which forces us to introduce into the analysis a principle which operates in a much more directly negative manner and to conceive a dimension of the Subject which is its dark side – the capacity also to embody evil or to seek pure pleasure in the destruction of the Other. We should add that without in any way intending to refer to themes of evil and negativity, everything concerning sexual-ity also deserves, as Maurice Godelier[40] suggests, to be examined in the light of a complex conception of the Subject, which does not restrict it to its dimensions of resistance to the powers that be and to norms or to its creativity, nor even, more broadly speaking, to its social dimensions.

De-subjectivization 'Touraine style' takes us back to the idea of a Subject which does not manage to exist: 'When I speak of the Subject, I begin by discussing the empty subject, crushed by the world of markets and communities, deper-sonalized and depressed.'[41] But other versions of the Subject must be added in particular to account for cruelty, violence for the sake of it, the pleasure derived from treating other people as non-Subjects, non-human beings, treating them like objects, or animals, as did, for example, the Nazi guards in Auschwitz, described by Primo Levi in his last book.[42] De-subjectivization taken to the extreme is an anti-subjectivization; it leads to genuine inversions and not only to a lack of subjectivity. It leads to figures of evil which are opposed to the image of the Subject to such an extent that it is possible to speak of them as anti-Subject. Rather than reduce the Subject to its oscillations from empty to over-full, or from the capacity of being an actor to the impossibility of ever being so, it is in our interest to adopt in our analyses a complex and richer definition of the Subject which includes its reverse side: the capacity or the potential of each individual to constitute him- or herself as an anti-actor and to participate actively, for example, in those anti-movements of which there is no lack in the world at the moment – terrorism, communitarianism, and so on.

By agreeing to be not only a sociology of the good, by opening up to this dimension of the anti-Subject, sociology can avoid a form of romanticism whereby the Subject is of necessity an attractive character, sometimes happy but usually unhappy; it leaves theoretical and practical scope for the darkest aspects of the human individual; it provides theoretical tools with which to embark on concrete research into phenomena as significant as racism, violence, or anti-Semitism.

Thinking globally

Just as 'Subject' has become an essential concept in all the social sciences, so too has 'globalization' since the 1980s. But in contrast to the term 'Subject', globalization has become commonplace in everyday speech and the media as well as in the field of research. Its fundamental characteristic is that its usage corresponds to two separate processes. On one hand, it is, in effect, descriptive and serves to account for the present or past state of the world, enabling us to depict historical reality. In this first usage, globalization is a material phenomenon, or a set of material phenomena which are economic, but also cultural and even ecological; it is the product of changes arising at a specific point in time and is the subject of important debates concerning the nature and intensity of these changes, as well as their date of occurrence, which enables us to situate them chronologically. On the other hand, the term has a conceptual usage; it serves to analyse problems in the present-day world, and to think about processes that are either new or being renewed and the forms of organization and disorganization that are (re)shaping social life. In this usage, 'globalization' is a tool for tackling the realities of our time.

Thus globalization refers at one and the same time to processes in the real world which the social sciences study and to a theoretical approach which should enable their study; it is the object and the tool with which to deal with this object. But this concept or tool is too often something of an all-purpose stereotype, even being presented almost as the ersatz of a general theory reduced in this instance to a single word which has become magic. This magic word, with no further explanation, is thought to suffice both to describe and to understand inequality, social injustice, the homogenization of culture and its fragmentation, the difficulties of states, and so on.

These two faces of 'globalization', its descriptive or historical use and its conceptual role, are in no way of equivalent scientific status. In one instance, globalization is an issue we have to familiarize ourselves with; in the other it is a concept which can assist our understanding. In the first instance, it is in the nature of a diagnosis – a diagnosis which is not unanimous. In the second, it is an approach, a way of apprehending the world. The two perspectives are distinct but difficult to separate: the more the world becomes 'globalized', the more we have to learn to think 'globally'.

The pre-history of the concept of globalization is undoubtedly to be found in Fernand Braudel and, in his wake, Immanuel Wallerstein, with his term the 'world-economy'.[43] According to this idea, at all times, throughout the history of humankind, economic systems have been constituted which extend far beyond the local framework or that of a restricted and well-defined territory, for example on the basis of a 'core-city' – 'world-economies'. But in fact it was in the 1980s that the idea of globalization became central, serving then to designate the creation of an interdependent global economic space and the omnipotence of financial and market capital functioning at world level and making light of states and frontiers.

Economics is the key

The ground was prepared in the 1970s by the rise in strength of liberal economic ideas; the first large-scale application of these at the level of a country was undoubtedly that of the Pinochet regime and, after the military coup in 1973, its invitation to the 'Chicago Boys', the students of the American economist Milton Friedman. The economic success of Chile could therefore be seen as the demonstration that political dictatorship and the market could very well go hand in hand.[44] Thereafter the coming to power of Ronald Reagan in the United States in 1980 and Margaret Thatcher in the United Kingdom in 1979 demonstrated the resounding success of liberal doctrines which were then to inform the policies of the major international financial institutions for the developing countries, namely the World Bank and the IMF. The first 'structural adjustment' plan concerned Senegal in 1979, and the fall of the Berlin Wall in 1989 led to the institution of 'shock therapies': for example, in Poland under the leadership of Leszek Balcerowicz.

The specificity of these economic policies and the thinking behind them was that they still fell entirely within the framework of the sovereign state, even if they were aided (or constrained) by the international institutions. It was a question of the ending of large-scale redistribution by the state, the liquidation or reduction of the welfare state, which did to a large extent exist in the Eastern European countries, to the benefit of the free play of the market – primarily the internal one – and the resort to drastic anti-inflationary measures.

On the ideological level, this liberal period prepared what was to follow but was not as yet classed in any way under 'globalization': action was thought of in the framework of the nation-state, and the economic forces which were to be freed up were those which were allegedly being stifled by it. It was a question of reducing the social role of the state and its direct economic influence, which was considered harmful, along the lines of an internal purge – in instances where 'globalization' was conveyed by planetary forces exerting their influence from outside the states. The transition from liberalism to neo-liberalism was to be located here.

At the outset, the idea of globalization referred in the very first instance to the image of an unavoidable economic phenomenon, impelled by the forces of financial and market capitalism and associated with the rise in strength of neo-liberal ideologies. At this stage, globalization meant the triumph of capitalism without borders, disregarding states and setting up open, global markets in which financial powers would no longer encounter any political obstacles. For Daniel Yergin and Joseph Stanislaw, for example,[45] globalization meant the supremacy of the market over state control, a process ongoing since Thatcher and Reagan, with privatization, deregulation, liberalization, and the institutional collapse of the world economic system as it had been organized since Bretton Woods.[46] From this point of view, globalization is the de-institutionalization of the world under the effect of economic forces – a de-institutionalization which nonetheless implied the functioning of institutions like the IMF and the World Bank, if only to provide and impose the doctrine which an economist, John Williamson, referred to in 1989 as the 'Washington consensus'.[47]

The movement of ideas in favour of these types of image gained momentum with the collapse of the Soviet bloc; the first clear expression of this process dates back to the coming to power in the USSR of Mikhail Gorbachev (1985) and his policy of *Glasnost* (transparency) and *Perestroika* (change). Thus, Francis Fukuyama says that the idea for the title of his highly successful book *The End of History and the Last*

Man – and therefore his conviction that the time had come for the universal triumph of democracy and the market – came to him at the very moment of the fall of the Berlin Wall in 1989. In this context, more widely, a powerful movement of ideas was constituted or gained momentum predicting the beginning of a new world order, the Cold War now having been cast aside. It was the period when many people wanted to believe in the unification of markets at world level, but also in the inevitable obsolescence of states, and in which there was an increasingly widespread recognition that the free circulation of capital enabled firms to locate their activities all over the world on the basis solely of their economic interests.

Throughout the 1990s there was a profusion of articles and publications, at the outset primarily by economists, some of whom were neo-liberal, others critical and anxious. Thus Robert Reich, close to Bill Clinton as his Minister for Labour, published *The Work of Nations: Preparing Ourselves for 21st Century Capitalism* in 1991,[48] describing a world in which the economy is stateless, with no national anchorage, where states lose their sovereignty and where there is no longer a political authority capable of rising up to confront the unbridled forces of capitalism, and where, thenceforth, there is a threat of anarchy, violence, and an absence of the rule of law. In France, the journalist Viviane Forrester's book *L'horreur économique*[49] was a cry of alarm, highly criticized by economists, but which had a considerable impact on public opinion.

It was not only economists who described what then appeared, finally, as the triumph of the economy over the political, and that of markets and technology over the state. Historians entered this march of ideas, in particular Paul Kennedy,[50] according to whom the challenges of the world in which we live – now finite – have ceased to be military and ideological and have become demographic, environmental, technological, and financial; if he is to be believed, the days of national policies and state intervention are over. Political scientists also intervened in the analysis of these changes. James Rosenau, in an oft-quoted book, speaks of 'turbulence'[51] to convey the idea that alongside the classical arena of international politics, the product of what is known as the 'Westphalian'[52] order, based on the diplomacy and action of national powers, there is a new one which will perhaps replace it where politics is not excluded, but is now transnational, acted out in an area where multinational firms, NGOs, and also institutions responsible for regulating relations all overlap. Not wishing to be outdone, sociologists and social anthropologists have introduced different images of globalization. These have become the focus of their analyses, the point of departure, or the descriptive tool of all types of cultural and political processes, not only economic ones.

All this does not mean that the idea of 'globalization' is unchallenged, or is established unanimously. For in the same historical context, an image which would appear to be very distant is emerging, in which the idea of a world united as a result of economic globalization is replaced by a world subject to fractures, breaks, and finally major conflicts. This is the 'clash of civilizations', a theme launched by the American political scientist Samuel Huntington in a resounding article, developed in 1996 into a book with this title, a bestseller at world level, and re-issued in 2000 with an immense impact since the attacks on 11 September 2001.[53] By concentrating on the idea of a conflict between Islam and the West, Huntington's hypothesis broke with the economism of the founding approaches of globalization and introduced culture and religion into the analysis, giving them pride of place. Should we now oppose 'globalization', a concept which ultimately unites (through the economy), to the 'clash of civilizations', a concept which, on the contrary, stresses conflict and even war? In fact in so doing we make two mistakes. The first is due to our own blindness: 'globalization', as demonstrated by the most critical publications as from the 1990s, produces all sorts of splits; the economic sphere becomes autonomous and in return gives rise to major phenomena of exclusion, of withdrawal into oneself, fragmentation of identity – and from this point of view, the 'clash of civilizations' is closely linked to the splits and rifts in question. The second mistake: Islam and the West do not necessarily maintain a non-relation, are not only defined by a 'clash'; there is also, as Nilüfer Göle[54] has shown, interpenetration, the presence of Islam in Western societies, modernization of Muslim societies, and not only in the form of radicalization, communitarianism, and violence.

The fact remains that when we take culture and religion into consideration, other conceptions of globalization emerge, in which it is not reduced to images of a wholly economic order.

The global and the local

For the Marxist geographer David Harvey,[55] the idea of globalization brings to mind the image of a 'dual time–space compression', the fact that henceforth, with modern communication tools, everything circulates at world level at an unbelievable speed; this type of approach opens up a vast space for reflection, raising spatial questions of territory and mobility, as well as those of culture, the way in which we live and construct our sense of belonging to an identity and our imaginations. From this point of view, technology plays a considerable role; in all sorts of fields, the network is going to be described as the form par excellence of organization of community life, whether it be the working of companies, or that of social movements or even of politics. If there exists a domain in which globalization is undeniable and oppressive, it is decidedly that of communications and surveillance. Is this domain controlled by the United States? Many believe so, either to denounce the present forms of American imperialism, the strength of its unilateralism, or, in more moderate fashion, to assert that globalization does have a centre and that it is not a multi-polar and multi-lateral phenomenon.

The fact remains that 'the information age',[56] to use the title of the forceful trilogy published by Manuel Castells, combines the most modern technologies of communication

and transport, based on micro-electronics, information technology, and digital telecommunications, with the multiplication of networks, within or between organizations and with
the networks of networks. Castells asserts that there is now
a dialectical tension between globalization and identity, and
between networks and individuals.

As we see in David Harvey's formula, space is not the only
factor and the analysis also involves time. Henceforth 'globalization' appears as a phenomenon reshaping our relationship to the past and the future, in particular by encouraging
what the historian François Hartog calls 'presentism', the
inability to think in terms of history and the tendency to
bring everything back to the present, while at the same time
promoting the 'nostalgia for the present' referred to by
Fredric Jameson.[57] In the words of Arjun Appadurai, the
social anthropologist, consumption has become 'the daily
practice through which nostalgia and fantasy are drawn
together in a world of commodified objects'.[58]

In addition to the images of economic forces without
borders, there are thus others which are more complex since
it is often a question of setting the individual and collective
experience of human beings in various spaces and in a revised
time frame. As a result, the sociologist Roland Robertson,
from the beginning of the 1990s, suggested that we speak
about 'glocalization': that is to say, the fact that modern
experience articulates global dimensions with others which
are local.[59]

The 'imagined communities' of cultural globalization

For Arjun Appadurai, according to Marc Abélès,[60] 'the
cultural dimension is at the centre of the process' of globalization, and he sees there the effect of a decisive phenomenon:
the explosion of the media, which 'has made possible
new and unpredictable expressions of the collective
imaginary'.[61]

This remark enables us to measure the distance travelled
since the 1980s, when Benedict Anderson, the historian and

social anthropologist, suggested thinking of the nation as a particular kind of construct, all the members of which share an 'imagined community' fashioned by printing and more particularly by the press, but also by the clock and the calendar.[62] Globalization, as it is analysed by Appadurai, is also effectively a question of 'imagined communities'. But these no longer function within the framework of the nation-state, as do Anderson's, whose research refers to historical periods other than our own. The approach suggested by Anderson is used, but on another scale than that of the nation and in another technological context: for Appadurai, the space of such imagined communities has now extended to the whole world as a result of television, the cinema, and the internet. We are therefore moving from the framework of the nation-state to that provided by the planet. It is composed of transnational public spheres, some of which are unstable, short-lived, lasting the time of an event, while others are fixed, of long duration, and structured by forms of solidarity. As Appadurai observes, these are 'public spheres of exiles' – in other words, diasporic networks whose publics are not confined within a frontier framework.

This thesis, which is brilliant, does have one drawback: it gives the impression that everyone is able to move around in a global, cultural arena and to belong to a diasporic network. In the globalization evoked here, each individual has multiple possibilities of re-appropriation of signs or cultural elements, whether they be borrowed from the dominant groups in the host society or originate elsewhere; it is a process open to all, of reinterpretation, of re-arrangement of the culture, and therefore highly favourable to creativity. The members of the new 'imagined communities' do not come within the remit of rationales of reproduction but of processes in which there is space for invention and new ideas. But this approach tells us nothing about those who are left to their own devices by these phenomena; all those who do not circulate, who are excluded from this world of mobility, and who nonetheless have global knowledge of the world through the images to which they have access.

The 'imaginary' is indeed increasingly 'global', whereas reality is not necessarily so, and therein lies, precisely, an essential dimension of globalization. This is what the economist Daniel Cohen[63] clearly explains when he observes that at the level of the planet, the worst drama for the countries in the Southern hemisphere, and for Africa in particular, is not so much being exploited as being ignored and considered useless – this is neatly compressed in the expression he quotes from Bernard Kouchner: 'The sick are in the South and the medicines are in the North.'[64] What is new with globalization is not so much the existence of these areas of poverty and exclusion, which are also found in rich countries, and sometimes in the very centre of the capitals; it is that the poor and the excluded, including in the most remote countries in the Southern hemisphere, have access to the global imaginary and to the virtual spectacle which is presented to the whole world and become acquainted, usually in real time, with images specific to the rich countries: '[T]he suburban life illustrates the novelty of the new world economy. Through the commuter railway or the movies, the suburbs of Paris, Cairo, Mexico, and China all evenly gaze upon the world. It is the world which ignores them.'[65]

An asymmetrical relationship thus characterizes globalization. Since the world is seen from everywhere and since it is formed of original communities, being imagined and at world level, on the one hand numerous individuals do not belong to any of these communities and, on the other, it does not suffice to have access to the sight of the images and symbols to be able to appropriate the content and the meaning. Discrepancies are created between awareness of the world and one's own existence, and between the imagined and real life, which can lead to intense frustration. This is an important source of Islamist radicalism and terrorism.

Globalization does not keep its promises. In Daniel Cohen's words:

> Globalization creates a strange world that nourishes the feeling of exploitation while in fact exploiting only a bit or

not at all. It creates an image of new closeness between
nations that is only virtual, not real. [. . .] It points both to
a deficit – the fact that the poorest are not integrated into
world capitalism – and to an excess – the presence of countries in the North as the obsessive horizon of economic
development.[66]

Globalization alters hopes and expectations all over the
world – without, however, increasing each individual's share
of its fruits, nor without necessarily developing the capacity
for action of individuals or peoples.

Thus consideration of the cultural and imagined dimensions of globalization leads us to break with over-simplistic,
purely economic, propositions which reduce it to the extension of the most unbridled forms of capitalism. The concept
which we can use to describe this term has to be complex:
it must take into account not only the processes of cultural
production which are at work, and the global imagination
or the 'imagined communities' which recognize each other
therein, but also the expectations, the frustrations, even the
heartbreak that these phenomena provoke. This is why religion fits perfectly into the frame of the major contemporary
realities which demand that we think 'globally'.

Discussing transnationalism

Consideration of the cultural dimensions of globalization
leads almost naturally to taking an interest in the major
question of migrations in the present-day world. For, contrary to what is suggested by a form of sociological misera-
bilism, migrants are not just a matter of dramatic images of
clandestine lives and what Michel Péraldi has called '*pater-
isme*': 'a vision combining compassion and condemnation
against a background conception of migratory movements
exclusively in terms of the police, even of criminals, focusing
attention and consideration on undocumented passengers
bound for Europe with no attention being paid to the plural-

ity of forms and the dynamics of circulation between the Maghreb, Africa, and Europe'.[67] The experience of migration is indeed often one of uprooting; it generally includes its lot of suffering and difficulties. But it is not uniquely that. Moreover, contrary to certain stereotypes, it does not necessarily lead to the distress of loss of identity, disappearance into mass or consumer society, the absorption of the migrant into the homogeneous culture of the cultural industries of the masses; it is also accompanied by the reproduction of cultural or religious forms and, even further, by the production of new cultural forms, linked to the ebb and flow of their comings and goings, de-territorialization, and mobility.

Henceforth, exoticism, which implies distance and exteriority, gives way to alterity, here and now. Migrants must be analysed from the point of view of their creativity and not only from that of their poverty and their difficulties; in cultural terms, and not only in their economic and social aspects, as well as from the point of view of their mobility. This, moreover, has been demonstrated in several recent exhibitions; these are often more informative than many learned publications.[68]

Today, a vast literature, often factual and devoted to the examination of precise situations, has put paid to over-simplistic ideas of migration that, on the whole, reduced it to a phenomenon in which groups and individuals leave their country of origin to end up in a host society, becoming absorbed there, after one or two generations, purely and simply in some sort of 'melting pot', or at least becoming integrated, retaining some specific cultural features, for example dietary customs. All over the world we can observe very different phenomena; here it suffices to say that they all have one major feature in common: mobility. All sorts of dynamics of circulation elude the deterministic and uniform model which only takes into consideration the departure from a country of origin and the arrival in a host society. The multiple and diverse nature of migratory phenomena is also a dimension of globalization. The fact is that all these movements of people take us back to social changes in the countries of origin, as in the countries of transition or reception, which are to a large extent due to disruptions inflicted or caused by economic globalization, processes of weakening of states in their capacity to control migratory flows, at the point of both departure and of arrival, as well as rationales of the circulation of money and goods which make light of borders and shape what Alejandro Portes and then Alain Tarrius have called 'globalization from below'.[69] Thus in the 1990s discussion began to take place around the notion of 'transnationalism'.

Not everything in this discussion is new. As far back as the 1960s one could hear people asking for consideration to be given to the subjective and cultural experience of migrants and their movements.[70] Similarly today the idea of 'transnationalism' refers to the mobility of the people concerned, to the fact that they move between two or more states, so much so that they become de-territorialized. Arjun Appadurai considers de-territorialization, in general, to be 'one of the central forces of the modern world because it brings laboring populations into the lower-class sectors and spaces of relatively wealthy societies, while sometimes creating exaggerated and intensified senses of criticism or attachment to politics in the home state'.[71] He adds, 'There is an urgent need to focus on the cultural dynamics of what is now called deterritorialization. This terms applies not only to obvious examples such as transnational corporations and money markets but also to ethnic groups, sectarian movements, and political formations, which increasingly operate in ways that transcend specific territorial boundaries and identities.'[72]

The concept of 'immigrant transnationalism' was first promoted by the social anthropologists Glick-Schiller, Basch, and Szanton-Blanc to account for what seemed to them to be a break with the past: the fact that migrants today maintain, construct, and reinforce multiple links with their countries of origin.[73] The expression then became fashionable and it is possible, over and above the nuances provided by various authors, to outline the key dimensions of a paradigm of transnationalism organized around five main points:

- [T]he process of migration and incorporation cannot be understood within the boundaries of a single state, whether this is the country of origin or the country of residence.
- [I]nstead of viewing migratory movements as necessarily unidirectional and non-recurring, they are viewed as potentially multiple and ongoing [. . .] and involve several countries.
- [M]igration and incorporation (what was traditionally referred to as 'settlement') are viewed as dynamic and interrelated processes.
- [The paradigm includes three levels of social scale.] These range from the level of individual actions and subjectivities to the mid level of community and local neighbourhoods and, finally, the macro-level of the nation.
- [The paradigm] does not necessarily privilege or prioritise a particular form of international relationship, such as economic or family ties and networks. Rather it provides scope for exploring their relevance alongside political, religious, educational and other linkages.[74]

The critique of transnationalism, for example in Roger Waldinger and David Fitzgerald,[75] in no way challenges the empirical observation, namely the fact that migrations are beginning to look like a plethora of forms of relations between countries of origin and countries of residence. It stresses that these relations cannot be understood without reference to the interventions of the states concerned, which have social and employment policies and control of national identity. They do maintain a degree of control over entry to and exit from the country and maintain relationships between states: migratory movements are subject to considerable constraints of a political type. Moreover, the notion of transnationalism should not be confused with that of internationalism. Migrants to whom transnationalism applies become members of new communities, perhaps even of a 'transnational civil society',[76] and, in the last resort, are defined outside any anchorage point within a national society, whether it be a sending or a receiving society; at a level above this type of belonging, a situation which may also have certain similarities with the absence of loyalty towards one state. Now, while this type of cosmopolitanism does exist, in particular amongst highly skilled workers or technicians with skills in high demand, and while there may be situations in which migrants invent their imagined community from start to finish, with no national bearings, and no connection with any sort of living community fixed within a state, this can only be one of many possible scenarios. Most of the time, migrants on the move combine or articulate their feelings of belonging, keeping special attachments here or there, while many others conform to the orthodox model of assimilation or integration. Moreover, critics question the novelty of the phenomenon which the concept of transnationalism claims to shed light on – apart from the increased possibilities for movement and communication offered by today's technologies for maintaining international relations and contacts cheaply, not everything here is new.

Globalization delineates economic and social spheres which no longer coincide with states and nations as before. What the notion of 'transnationalism' has come to mean is movement, of various sorts, of migrants within this type of space. And contrary to what the metaphor of 'fluidity' dear to the heart of Zygmunt Bauman might lead us to believe, this movement is not fluid everywhere or for everyone. Thus obstacles and bottlenecks are created in the vicinity of some frontiers which are apparently sealed and closely guarded (road blocks, barbed wire, miradors, etc.) where the migratory flows are considerable and where intense commercial activities both legal and illegal develop; some are also even industrial and controlled by the production demands of the globalized economy. One example is the *maquiladoras*, those factories set up by the most 'global' capital in existence in Mexico and, at the outset at least, close to the frontier with the United States. Situations of this type are the product –

paradoxical as it may be – of globalization and the resistance of states.

But the discussion on transnationalism should not be confined to its social and cultural dimensions. As James Beckford observes, with astonishment, 'the sociologists who are known for their work on globalization [with the notable exception of Roland Robertson and Peter Beyer, he specifies] tend [he quotes Albrow, Beck, Castells, Harvey] to have very little interest in religion. This silence (or else this lack of interest) is all the more astonishing as religion represents a particularly stimulating case for the specialists of globalization.'[77] Religion has been global for a very long time. But its recent transformations have involved its participation in a new era characterized by the increasing complexity and density of networks, the multiplication of interconnections, and the growing role of transnational religious actors. The centres for the dissemination of various religions are becoming multiple; not only do the faithful participate in local processes of hybridization or syncretism, but they also move from one religion to another with increasing ease. The global processes of expansion and circulation of religions are increasingly multilateral and are increasingly part of economic strategies or calculations. Pentecostalisms, for example, 'more than any other movement, radicalize the Protestant rationale of the independent religious entrepreneur-cum-leader whose image is central to processes of globalization'.[78] The Afro-Brazilian religions are also becoming globalized, they are being de-territorialized, they are becoming separated from their original anchorages and becoming utilitarian; they are judged in terms of their efficacy on the highly competitive market of magico-religious goods. They are changing 'from a communitarian event, the expression of an identity lived out in the warmth and stimulation of a homogeneous ethnic and social group, into an abstract product, targeting an abstract market, formed by people of various ethnic, social and national origins'.[79] In this context, religion is becoming a market offer and moving away from the classical institutions (this is particularly clear with Catholicism) while at the same time increasingly resorting to the modern media. Furthermore, its globalization is also a phenomenon which is ceasing to be associated with the political hegemonies in certain states, as was the case during European colonial expansion.

The re-institutionalization of the world

Discussion in the 1990s often appeared to be a confrontation between two camps: the 'friends' and the 'enemies' of economic globalization, its theoretical or ideological foundations (neo-liberalism) and its consequences. The 'enemies' developed various critiques:[80] globalization was a source of weakening of states and of loss of sovereignty; one of its consequences was the reinforcement of inequalities between countries and within countries; it eroded social welfare and everything associated with the welfare state. It created strong pressure on wage earners, imposing shareholders' demands for short-term profitability and, as a result, vulnerability, and ended productivity-related salary increases. Furthermore, it was a factor in cultural homogenization and, consequently, in cultural impoverishment given the effect of mass consumption. The uniformization which it implied could penetrate the world of work and firms, as George Ritzer demonstrated concerning the generalization of the methods of management and organization implemented by McDonald's – what he called the 'McDonaldization of society'.[81] At the same time, and this is not contradictory, it was a source of cultural fragmentation, linked to the fears and frustrations which it produced and which resulted in tendencies to withdrawal into various forms of communitarianism including those associated with identity, religion, and nationalism. Sometimes the criticism was backed up by a denunciation of American imperialism, as if the two phenomena – hegemony or the domination of the United States, on one hand, and globalization, on the other – were one and the same thing.

The defence of globalization sometimes took the form of a plea for 'happy globalization', in the words of Alain Minc, since, if we are to believe him, it creates wealth which can benefit everyone. More sophisticated analyses also came to the fore, demanding an end to the reduction of globalization to over-simplistic images of an advance of the forces of money without borders or regulation. Instead pleas were made for consideration to be given to the novelty constituted by the creation of a transnational political and legal sphere which was not a substitute for the classical spheres of the Westphalian era but an addition thereto and for the world to be considered in concrete terms, as it was. Thus Elie Cohen[82] asks us to think about the different levels of government and political action involved and to cease making of the transnational or supranational sphere a new vacuum. The problem is one of the articulation of 'world, regional and local levels of government [. . .]. How', asks Cohen, 'can we combine regulation and governance in a world which is ever more open to exchanges?'[83] How in the very first instance can we regulate market exchanges? Cohen asks questions about the 'problems of institutional engineering' which have to be resolved to 'reconcile market rationales, social and environmental constraints, and the conservation of cultural diversity'.[84]

Concerns of this sort are increasingly frequent in publications at the beginning of the twenty-first century. Pascal Lamy, for example, at the time European Commissioner for Trade, asked questions about methods enabling the harmonization of the process of globalization and therefore of free trade, and the open economy, with national processes for collective preference – in other words, the fact that each country makes choices and has its own identity, its values, its 'collective preferences', for example in environmental matters, the death penalty, food safety regulations, recognition of cultural diversity, public service, and so on.[85]

Above all, the analysis is gradually striving to understand the working of supranational spaces. By ceasing to be set mainly, if not exclusively, within the framework of the nation-states and their relations alone, the social sciences are distancing themselves from the way in which they were, on the whole, founded and institutionalized. They are learning to become more independent and are opening up new perspectives. Thus, in particular, traditional international relations are giving way to completely new viewpoints: 'The classical conception of international relations is based on this clear distinction between what happens within states, which pertains to sociological analysis, and what happens in the outside world, which is considered to be above society and would explain the exteriority of the international in relation to the social.'[86] Today, sociology conceives of spaces, forms of action, or social relationships which are encroaching on the traditional space of 'international relations', putting an end to the quasi-monopoly of states, formerly the only actors in this sphere. Some researchers are interested in the cultural or social actors who are the driving forces behind the new supranational spaces – NGOs of all sorts or alter-globalization movements;[87] others in the actors of economic regulation and their real functioning, for example the World Trade Organization (WTO). Elie Cohen, referring to the WTO, the IMF, or the European Central Bank, says 'there is a proto-economic government at world level'.[88]

Consideration has also been given to legal aspects: what sort of world law should be constructed, not so much in opposition to states but to ensure that they are not left with the monopoly of settling everything in legal matters? Mireille Delmas-Marty's books, in particular, show how the growing influence of judges and a form of supranational law accompany fragmentation and loss of efficiency in national legislative and executive powers. She says there is a 'jurisdic-tionalization of international law' and a 'rise in the power of judges', even if for the time being nothing seems to be possible without the good willing of states, for example for the International Court of Justice.[89] There are now European Courts, United Nations Committees (beginning with the UN Human Rights Committee), appeal institutions like the one set up by the WTO, arbitration centres, and penal tribunals like the International Tribunal for the Law of the Sea – in short, a jurisdictional sphere is being constituted and is getting denser. It has even been said that, in general, progress in human rights come from outside states, as with the 'right to intervention'. Thus Seyla Benhabib observes that 'the civil and social rights of migrants, foreigners, and residents are increasingly protected by international texts concerning human rights'.[90] The 'right to have rights', in Hannah Arendt's resounding phrase, is no longer dictated uniquely by states and their agreements; we are witnessing the coming of cosmopolitan norms in matters of human rights but also in commercial or economic law. A form of 'global' law is being created which is no longer controlled by the states alone and which no longer owes everything to their deliberations or the work of their parliaments and which is developing as a result of the effect of agreements in which NGOs, major firms, international agencies, and so on, may intervene. Thus, for example, the labour employed by multinational firms is subject to rules fixed by these firms, much more than to the law of the states in which they work; as it happens, this more frequently leads to vulnerability and situations of over-exploitation than to over-protection of the labour in question. Territories are delinking and dislocating and law is also becomes trans- or supranational.

But in the expansion of global justice and law, we should not under-estimate the impact of grass-roots mobilization, conveyed by social movements, humanitarian actors, scientists, charitable organizations, which have an impact on public opinion, even through restricted and highly localized action, via the media, and, from there, on the working of law and justice at supranational level, as Fuyuki Kurasawa has demonstrated in an important book.[91]

It is therefore wrong to state that globalization forces the whole world into the de-institutionalized rationale of world-level markets without frontiers and of financial flows. Not only does trade remain dominated by relations of proximity but also, and above all, forms of regulation, systems of actors, and legal norms are set up or develop which fill the supranational space. At the outset, globalization was perceived as the rupture between the all-powerful forces of the economy and the forms of collective life, which recalls what Marx said of the capitalism of his time when he stated that the development of the forces of production was separating from the relations of production. But globalization also includes the contrary of this rationale of rupture; it is flexible and to some extent also arises from the construction of institutions and the interplay of actors which make it viable. This is why research like that of the geographer Michel Foucher leads to an image of the phenomenon which is no longer that of the triumph of markets and pure capitalism over states, but is much closer to that of a reorganization, at world level, of states and their frontiers. 'Since 1991,' notes Foucher, 'more than 26,000 kilometres of new international frontiers have been created, a further 24,000 have been the subject of agreements for delimitation and demarcation, and if the projects published for walls, fences and metal barriers were all completed, they would stretch for over 18,000 kilometres'. Foucher considers that the Westphalian model is vital, a 'dialectic of economic overture and territorial consolidation' is being implemented, and the 'fetish word of globalization' may well conceal the main point: the geopolitical reorganization of the world.[92]

This reorganization does not only appear in its positive guise, that of a re-institutionalization in which various actors construct a space which is preferable to the vacuum or the chaos of the jungle. It also has its dark side: the re-institutionalization of torture, with the United States leading the way at Guantanamo Bay. Organized crime has also been globalized, while major international organizations have been discredited time and again. How can we forget that the UN Human Rights Committee was, for a while, presided over by Colonel Gaddafi? We cannot accept the naïve image of the completely harmonious institutionalization of the supranational space, at once gradual and progressive.

The end of globalization?

Right from the beginning of the 1990s, with the terrible violence in ex-Yugoslavia, the idea of globalization, at least in its initial formulation, was weakened given the predominance of nationalism, war, and state intervention. Awareness of the return of this political order was also undoubtedly prepared and accelerated by the difficulties of the most global capitalism in existence to date, with a number of scandals in the United States in particular, highlighting the corruption which could occur at the centre of world capitalism. In addition, social themes concerning social injustice, exclusion, and the reinforcement of inequality returned to public discussion. 'Happy' globalization appeared to be purely mythical and ceased to inform the discourse of the leaders of the major international institutions, the IMF and the World Bank: the 'Washington consensus' has long since been replaced by the realization that in the absence of regulation, intervention in a supranational public sphere, and the ability of states to act, the world economy was vulnerable to crises – even at local level.

With the attacks on 11 September 2001 it was quite clear that the world had entered a new era. This had in fact been inaugurated earlier, as we saw in chapter 3. But suddenly, war, imperialism, the perspective of the 'clash of civilizations' popularized by Samuel Huntington, all clearly indicated that the world was not united by neo-liberalism, or the new capitalism, and that politics, war, or diplomacy and the interplay of states were on the agenda. A new historical phase opened, in which the return of the political–military order replaced the apparent triumph of the economy; the resort to force and the assertion of states replaced the cosmopolitanism of money. After the '9/11' attacks the United States, followed by other states, declared war on terrorism; they started military intervention in Afghanistan, and then got bogged down in the war in Iraq. The question of Israeli–Palestinian relations and the war in Lebanon did the rest and marked the return of states, of war, diplomacy, and politics. Everyone agreed that the 'economics is the key' approach of the 1990s was outdated; globalization was not the only motive force in the world and it had perhaps lost its centrality.

In this new climate of opinion, one of the major dimensions of the idea of globalization, namely the assertion that it is linked to the inevitable decline of the form of the nation-state, has been increasingly vigorously criticized, to the point sometimes of being reversed. Thus the Africanist Jean-François Bayart questions the image of triumphant globalization; he points out that with regard to the circulation of labour, and therefore of people, or property rights, which remain inscribed in national structures, 'contemporary capitalism is far from being global'.[93] Pushing the criticism even further, Bayart overturns generally accepted ideas and states that globalization is the interweaving of transnational relations, including the market of the economists, with the process of state formation: 'Globalization is not the outcome of the overdevelopment of transnational relations (or of the market) at the expense of the state, as maintained at first glance by the theoreticians of international relations or the international political economy. It is the synthesis of these apparently contradictory principles.'[94] For good measure, he adds that the historical matrix of globalization dates not from the 1970s but from the nineteenth century.

As we can see, on all sides the idea of globalization as a concrete historical reality is either criticized or else presented as much more complex than the over-simple idea which reduces it to an unprecedented expansion of financial or market capital, sweeping aside obstacles and making light of nation-states and their frontiers. Some speak of the end of globalization, of the decline of what is then presented as an ideology which had its hour of glory for a decade from the fall of the Berlin Wall to the '9/11' attacks. In economic matters, we should henceforth acknowledge that the concept is outmoded, that the criticisms which have just been evoked weigh heavier in the balance than the opposite points of view, and that the affirmation of China and India in the world economy is not being implemented in a global mode but according to processes of action specific to the capitalism of these 'emerging' countries. Has the time not come to proclaim the 'collapse of globalism', to use the title of John Saul's book?[95] If it is a question of demonstrating the ideological nature of those rather unrefined discourses which proclaimed the inevitable, and desirable, entry into an era where only the forces of financial capital counted, it would be preferable to stop talking about globalization. But just because the world economy bears little correspondence today to the most summary images of globalization does not justify our abandoning the idea and the term. On the contrary, the best economic analyses invite us to envisage the present period as the one in which, truly, the facts are coming closer to the concept – particularly if one agrees to recognize that globalization is not necessarily synonymous with the decline of states.

Thus Michel Aglietta and Laurent Berrebi recently demonstrated that the Asian crisis in 1997 'provoked a radical change in the interdependencies which structure the world economy'.[96] Until then, globalization was primarily the protection of Western, and *de facto* American, capitalism in the world; in a way the word designated a form of domination, according to the terms of which the centre (the United States, at the height of the 'Washington consensus') indicated to the emerging countries the reforms which they had to make to receive foreign investment. But now 'the emerging countries have recovered their sovereignty over their economic and strategic choices'.[97] They exert considerable influence over developed economies, they have their own dynamics, their financial weight, and they export goods. The world economy is organized from several centres – there are at least three, the United States, Europe, and Asia; it is becoming multipolar. Thus it is now possible to propose a complex concept of globalization, instead of it being a poor and simplifying descriptive category.

In the first instance this concept consists of a suggestion that we refuse the monopoly of the 'Westphalian' frame of reference for the analysis (to use the adjective popularized by Roseneau) and that, like Ulrich Beck,[98] we challenge 'methodological nationalism', which consists in tackling problems uniquely from a national perspective. It is not a question of choosing between classical approaches giving preference to the framework of the nation-state and global or transnational approaches, but – and this is much more delicate – of understanding the links, the ways in which what belongs to each overlap and how to unravel them. Saskia Sassen writes that at the centre of globalization there is a 'proliferation of new arrangements. Fragments of territory, of authority and of rights which were formerly part of more diffuse institutional domains, located within the nation-state or sometimes within the supranational system, are reassembled within specific, partial and highly specialized arrangements directed towards special aims and uses.'[99] Thinking globally means integrating into the analysis processes of destructuration/restructuration; it means articulating the internal and the external, global or transnational processes and internal, national even local processes, by taking into consideration the 'dual time–space compression', to use David Harvey's phrase quoted above. This also implies not restricting globalization to its economic aspects alone, integrating the world of symbols and make-believe into the concept, giving full rein to culture; many of our relations to the world are indeed constructed in imaginative mode, even those which are rooted and localized. Today's imaginative world is global and planet-wide whereas yesterday's was national. Globalization is not a phenomenon with one-dimensional and highly foreseeable consequences; it is not an inexorable fate which would make of the concept a new philosophy of history. It combines various processes, and various dimensions, without our ever being able to speak of '*one best way*' (or rather '*one worst way*') for humankind. We have to learn to think globally more and more systematically, and therefore to use a complex concept of globalization, which is not the same thing as proposing a diagnosis of the state of the world – but which obviously in no way excludes this.

This type of concept, as we demonstrated on the subject of violence, terrorism, and racism, enables us to shed considerable light on phenomena which fall within the domain of evil. It enables us to improve our understanding and, at the same time, to set it at the highest level of generality, the level at which it is appropriate for us to be located to tackle the majority of the major problems of the present-day world.

*

By thinking 'global', on one hand, and by focusing on the subjectivity of the actors, and on the processes of subjectivization and de-subjectivization which may lead them to paths of evil, on the other, we are going well beyond the classical analyses. These usually restrict the study of globalization to its economic and possibly cultural dimensions, just as they reduce the Subject to the somewhat romanticized aspects of its capacity to act.

Tackling violence, terrorism, and racism other than by moral and incantatory speechifying or by repressive practices which never themselves solve the problems means stretching theory to a breaking point and envisaging in one and the same movement both their most global content as well as their most subjective message.

Understanding evil, like understanding good, necessarily implies endeavouring to reconcile the seemingly irreconcilable.

Notes

Preface

1 Michel Wieviorka, *Neuf leçons de sociologie* (Paris: Robert Laffont, 2008).

Chapter 1 Facing Evil: A Sociological Perspective

1 Alain Touraine, *A New Paradigm for Understanding Today's World* (Cambridge: Polity, 2007), p. 94.
2 Paul Ricoeur, 'Ethique appliquée', in *Dictionnaire d'éthique et de philosophie morale*, Vol. 1 (Paris: Presses Universitaires de France, 2004) p. 694.
3 Anthony David Smith, *The Ethnic Revival* (Cambridge: Cambridge University Press, 1981).
4 Jean-Michel Chaumont, *La concurrence des victimes: génocide, identité, reconnaissance* (Paris: La Découverte, 1997).
5 Hannah Arendt, *Eichmann in Jerusalem: A Report on the Banality of Evil* (New York: Viking Press, 1963; revised and enlarged edition, 1968).

Chapter 2 An End to Violence

1 André Lalande, *Vocabulaire technique et critique de la philosophie* (Paris: Presses Universitaires de France, 1968). 'When

we, who live under civil laws, are compelled to make some contract not required by law, we can, thanks to the law, set aside violence.' Montesquieu, *De L'Esprit des Lois* (1758), livre XXVI, chap. XX, in *Œuvres complètes*, II (Paris: Gallimard, 1985 [Bibliothèque de la Pléiade]), p. 773.

2 Cf. Sami Makki, *Militarisation de l'humanitaire, privatisation du militaire* (Paris: CIRPES, 2004). In 2005, 45,000 civilians employed by 453 'contractors' provided support services for a force of 145,000 men and carried out activities some of which normally fell to the state – questioning prisoners or suspects, for example.

3 Alexis de Tocqueville, *The Old Regime and the Revolution: The Complete Text*, Vol. I (Chicago and London: University of Chicago Press, 2004 [1856]), p. 222.

4 Cf., for example, Ted Robert Gurr (ed.), *Handbook of Political Conflict* (New York: Free Press, 1980).

5 Norbert Elias, *The Civilizing Process, Vol. I: The History of Manners* (Oxford: Blackwell, 1969 [1939]), and *The Civilizing Process, Vol. II: State Formation and Civilization* (Oxford: Blackwell, 1982 [1939]).

6 Theodor Adorno, Else Frenkel-Brunswik, Daniel Levinson and Nevitt Sanford, *The Authoritarian Personality* (New York: Harper, 1960).

7 Hannah Arendt, *Eichmann in Jerusalem: A Report on the Banality of Evil* (New York: Viking Press, 1963; revised and enlarged edition, 1968).

8 In Michel Wieviorka, *Violence: A New Approach* (London: Sage, 2009).

9 Stanley Milgram, *Obedience to Authority: An Experimental View* (London: Tavistock, 1974).

10 Human Security Centre, *Human Security Report 2005* (Vancouver and New York: Oxford University Press, 2006).

11 Charles Tilly proposes this concept in *The Contentious French* (Cambridge, Mass.: Belknap Press of Harvard University Press, 1986), explaining that any population, in a given society, at a given period, has a limited set of collective actions, that is to say, means of acting in concert on the basis of shared interest. That repertoire changes as one moves from one type of society to another.

12 Richard Sennett, 'Récits au temps de la précarité', in Michel Wieviorka with Aude Debarle and Jocelyne Ohana (eds), *Les*

sciences sociales en mutation (Auxerre: Éditions Sciences Humaines, 2007), p. 437.

13 Cf. the thesis of Luis Ernesto Lopez, *En quête d'identité: Mondialisation, figures de la féminité et conflits sociaux à la frontière Mexique/États-Unis* (Paris: École des Hautes Études en Sciences Sociales, 2007).

14 Norbert Elias, *Reflections on a Life* (Cambridge: Polity Press, 1994 [1990]).

15 Bill Clinton, *My Life* (London: Hutchinson, 2004), pp. 782–3.

16 Olivier Pétré-Grenouilleau, *Les traites négrières: Essai d'histoire globale* (Paris: Gallimard, 2004).

17 Dipesh Chakrabarty, 'Histoire et politique de la reconnaissance', in Wieviorka et al. (eds), *Les sciences sociales en mutation*.

18 Jacques Derrida, 'Le siècle et le pardon', conversation with Michel Wieviorka, *Le monde des débats* (December 1999).

19 See the analyses in Michel Wieviorka (ed.), *Le printemps du politique* (Paris: Robert Laffont, 2007).

20 Cf. notably John Dower, *War without Mercy: Race and Power in the Pacific* (New York: Pantheon Books, 1986).

21 Jean Bergeret, *Freud, la violence et la dépression* (Paris: Presses Universitaires de France, 1995), p. 46.

Chapter 3   Global Terrorism

1 I am relying here in particular on my publications: *The Making of Terrorism* (Chicago: University of Chicago Press, 1993; new edition, 2003); *Face au terrorisme* (Paris: Liana Lévi, 1995); and with Dominique Wolton, *Terrorisme à la Une* (Paris: Gallimard, 1987).

2 Albert Camus, *The Rebel* (Harmondsworth: Penguin, 2000 [1951]).

3 See note 1 above.

4 Boris Savinkov, *Memoirs of a Terrorist* (New York: Albert & Charles Boni, 1931 [1909]).

5 Jean-Paul Brodeur, 'Que dire maintenant de la police?', lecture delivered on the occasion of a homage in memory of Dominique Monjardet, Paris, 2006

6 Michel Wieviorka, 'Defining and Implementing Foreign Policy: The US Experience in Anti-Terrorism', in Yonah Alexander and Abraham H. Foxman (eds), *The 1988–1989 Annual on*

Terrorism (Dordrecht: Kluwer Academic Publishers, 1990), pp. 71–201; cf. also Wieviorka, 'France Faced with Terrorism', *Studies in Conflict and Terrorism*, 14(3), 1991, 157–70.

7 Cf., for example, Gary R. Bunt, *Islam in the Digital Age* (London: Pluto Press, 2003).

8 Cf., for example, John Robb, *Brave New War: The Next Stage or Terrorism and the End of Globalization* (Hoboken, NJ: John Wiley and Sons, 2007).

9 Cf., for example, Robert Pape, who advances the figures of 95 per cent in 'The Strategic Logic of Suicide Terrorism', *The American Political Science Review*, 97(3), 346–50. And, by the same author, the frequently quoted book *Dying to Win: The Strategic Logic of Suicide Terrorism* (New York: Random House, 2005).

10 André Glucksmann, *Dostoïevski à Manhattan* (Paris: Robert Laffont, 2002).

11 Hans Magnus Enzensberger, *Le perdant radical: Essai sur les hommes de la terreur* (Paris: Gallimard, 2006), pp. 29–30.

12 Ibid., p. 31.

13 In Ulrich Beck, *Cosmopolitan Vision* (Cambridge: Polity Press, 2006).

14 Farhad Khosrokhavar, *Suicide Bombers: Allah's New Martyrs* (London: Pluto Press, 2005 [2002]).

15 In her preface to Zahida Kakachi and Christophe Morin, *Le vol Alger-Marseille: Journal d'otages* (Paris: Plon, 2006), pp. 14–15.

16 Ibid., p. 15. Cf. also Françoise Rudetzki, *Triple peine* (Paris: Calmann-Lévy, 2004).

17 'Suicide bombing is the signature tactic of the fourth or "religious wave" of modern terrorism', in the words of the opening lines of the preface by the editor to an important book devoted to the subject. 'No contemporary terrorist method is more important to understand.' Ami Pedahzur (ed.), *Root Causes of Suicide Terrorism: The Globalization of Martyrdom* (London: Routledge, 2006), p. xv.

18 Farhad Khosrokhavar, *Quand Al Qaïda parle: Témoignages derrière les barreaux* (Paris: Grasset, 2006). The 'Islamo-nihilist' has no roots and is 'searching for an Islam which provides an existential answer to the feeling of misfortune which overcomes him' (p. 332). The 'Islamo-plethorist' has 'a much more extensive religious grounding'; he is educated, he

gives 'a religious meaning to the totality of the acts' of his existence (pp. 334–5). The 'Islamo-individualist' would like to live as a believer and an individual and challenges the West, which makes it impossible for him to make this dream come true. Finally, the 'Islamo-fundamentalist' comes from a neo-communitarian group which has inculcated into him a 'closed conception of the world of religion' (p. 344). He goes from fundamentalism, usually a calming influence, to terrorism as a result of a radicalization which is due to humiliation or to repression.

19 Khosrokhavar, *Suicide Bombers*, p. 226.
20 Saskia Sassen, *The Global City* (Princeton, NJ: Princeton University Press, 1991; updated second edition, 2001).
21 Marc Sageman, 'Islam and al Qaeda', in Pedahzur (ed.), *Root Causes of Suicide Terrorism*, p. 127.

Chapter 4   The Return of Racism

1 Cf., for France, Michel Wieviorka, *The Lure of Anti-Semitism: Hatred of Jews in Present-Day France* (Leiden and Boston: Brill, 2007 [2005]).
2 Let me refer the reader here to my survey on *La France raciste* (Paris: Seuil, 1991) and its companion volume *Le racisme en Europe* (Paris: La Découverte, 1993).
3 In their book *Black Power: The Politics of Liberation* (New York: Vintage Books, 1967).
4. Philippe Bataille, *Le racisme au travail* (Paris: La Découverte, 1999).
5 Cf. Michel Wieviorka, *Neuf leçons de sociologie* (Paris: Robert Laffont, 2008), chapter 3.
6 On all these questions, permit me to refer the reader to my book *Le racisme: Une introduction* (Paris: La Découverte, 1998).
7 Cf. in particular Loïc Wacquant and William Wilson, 'The Cost of Racial and Class Exclusion in the Inner City', *The Annals of the American Academy of Political and Social Science*, January 1989, 8–25. See also on these questions, William J. Wilson, *The Truly Disadvantaged: The Inner City, the Underclass and Public Policy* (Chicago: University of Chicago Press, 1987).

8 Dinesh D'Souza, *The End of Racism* (New York: Free Press, 1995).

9 Joe Feagin and Melvin Sikes, *Living with Racism* (Boston: Beacon, 1994).

10 Cf. Alexandra Poli, *L'expérience vécue du racisme et des discriminations raciales en France: D'une condamnation morale à la prise en charge de la subjectivité des victimes*, thesis for doctorate in sociology (Paris: EHESS, 2006).

11 Cf. the clarification set out by John Wrench, *Diversity Management and Discrimination* (Aldershot: Ashgate, 2007).

12 The idea of the self-fulfilling prophecy, which the social sciences owe to William Isaac Thomas, was popularized by Robert Merton. The idea is that a false representation of the real world exerts effects which result in modifying the reality in the direction which it suggests.

13 Christian Jelen, *Les casseurs de la République* (Paris: Plon, 1997).

14 Cf. the studies by Della Pergola and Doris Bensimon, *La population juive de France: Socio-démographie et identité* (Paris: Éditions du CNRS, 1984), or those of Erik Cohen, *Le Juifs de France: Valeurs et identités* (Paris: FSJU, 2002).

15 Livio Sansone, 'Anti-Racism in Brazil', *NACLA Report on the Americas*, vol. 38, no. 2, Sept.–Oct. 2004

16 The term 'negritude' was coined by Aimé Césaire and its concept clarified after the Second World War by Léopold Sédar Senghor.

17 Peter Schäfer, *Judeophobia: Attitudes toward the Jews in the Ancient World* (Cambridge, Mass. and London: Harvard University Press, 1997).

18 Georges Felouzis, Françoise Liot, and Joëlle Perroton, *L'apartheid scolaire: Enquête sur la ségrégation ethnique dans les collèges* (Paris: Seuil, 2005).

19 Cf. Charles P. Henry, *Long Overdue: The Politics of Racial Reparations* (New York: New York University Press, 2007), in particular chapter 5, with the explicit title: 'Reparations Go Global'.

20 Pierre Bourdieu and Loïc Wacquant, 'Sur les ruses de la raison impérialiste', *Actes de la Recherche en Sciences Sociales*, 121–2, 1998, 109–18. The Brazilian journal *Estudos Afro-Asiaticos* and the British journal *Theory, Culture & Society* republished this article and conducted a discussion on it. See

Bourdieu and Wacquant, 'On the Cunning of Imperialist Reason', *Theory, Culture & Society*, 16(1), 1999, 41–58.

21 Claude Lévi-Strauss, 'Race and History', in *Structural Anthropology*, Vol. II (New York: Basic Books, 1976), pp. 323–62.

22 Cf. François Hartog, *Évidence de l'histoire* (Paris: Gallimard, 2007 [2005]), p. 235, who refers to 'this preoccupation with time, that is, with various modes of temporality, which I now refer to as systems of historicity'.

23 Cf. Wieviorka, *Neuf leçons de sociologie*, chapter 3.

24 Published under the title *L'Allemagne nazie et le génocide juif* (Paris: Gallimard/Le Seuil, 1982).

Chapter 5   The New Arena of the Social Sciences, or: How to Raise the Level of Generalization

1 Jean-Paul Sartre, *Search for a Method* (New York: Vintage Books, 1968 [1960]), p. 91.

2 Albert Hirschman, *Shifting Involvements: Private Interest and Public Action* (Princeton, NJ: Princeton University Press, 1982).

3 Alain Touraine, *What is Democracy?* (Boulder, Colo.: Westview Press, 1994), p. 12.

4 Eric J. Hobsbawm and Terence O. Ranger (eds), *The Invention of Tradition* (Cambridge: Cambridge University Press, 1983).

5 David Le Breton, *Passions du risque* (Paris: Métailié, 2004).

6 Philippe Bataille, 'Mourir sans partir: L'impossible statut de mourant', in Michel Wieviorka with Aude Debarle and Jocelyne Ohana (eds), *Les sciences sociales en mutation* (Auxerre: Éditions Sciences Humaines, 2007), pp. 91–101; *Un cancer et la vie: Les malades face à la maladie* (Paris: Éditions Balland, 2001).

7 Alain Ehrenberg, *The Weariness of the Self: Diagnosing the History of Depression in the Contemporary Age* (Montreal: McGill-Queen's University Press, 2009 [1998]).

8 François de Singly, *Libres ensembles* (Paris: Nathan, 2000).

9 Cf., for example, the evaluation of the research published by Heather Beth Johnson, 'From the Chicago School to the New Sociology of Children: The Sociology of Children and Childhood in the United States, 1900–1999', *Advances in Life Course Research*, 6, 1999, 53–93.

10 François Dubet and Danilo Martuccelli, *À l'école: Sociologie de l'expérience scolaire* (Paris: Seuil, 1996).
11 Judith Butler, *Gender Trouble: Feminism and the Subversion of Identity* (New York: Routledge, 1990), p. 2.
12 Georges Friedmann, *The Anatomy of Work: Labor, Leisure and the Implications of Automation* (New Brunswick, NJ: Transaction, 1992 [1956]).
13 Horst Kern and Michael Schumann, *Das Ende der Arbeitstellung?* (Munich: Beck, 1984).
14 Dominique Méda, *Le travail: Une valeur en cours de disparition* (Paris: Aubier, 1995), p. 300. Cf. also Jeremy Rifkin, *The End of Work: The Decline of the Global Labor Force and the Dawn of the Post-Market Era* (New York: Putnam, 1997).
15 Richard Sennett, *The Corrosion of Character: The Personal Consequences of Work in the New Capitalism* (New York: W.W. Norton, 1998) and *The Culture of the New Capitalism* (New Haven: Yale University Press, 2005).
16 Cf. Marie-France Hirigoyen, *Stalking the Soul: Emotional Abuse and the Erosion of Identity* (New York: Helen Marx Books, 2000 [1998]).
17 Michel Lallement, *Le travail: Une sociologie contemporaine* (Paris: Gallimard, 2007), p. 545.
18 Ibid., p. 546.
19 Cf. Daniel Bertaux, 'Alternatives conceptuelles sur la question du sujet dans la sociologie française', in Roberto Cipriani (ed.), *Aux sources des sociologies de langue française et italienne* (Paris: L'Harmattan, 1997), which refers to his own research but also to the studies of Montaldi, Revelli, Ferrarotti, Campelli, Cipriani, Macioti, d'Amato Cavallaro, and so on.
20 Cf. Alain Touraine, *Thinking Differently* (Cambridge: Polity Press, 2009 [2007]); Bruno Latour, *Changer de société, refaire de la sociologie* (Paris: La Découverte, 2006).
21 With Pierre Bourdieu, the idea of *habitus* is tempered by that of field, developed elsewhere, since in a 'field' *à la* Bourdieu, there is space for the interplay of rival actors. Cf. Bertaux, 'Alternatives conceptuelles sur la question du sujet dans la sociologie française'.
22 Pierre Bourdieu, *Masculine Domination* (Cambridge: Polity Press, 2001 [1998]). Alain Touraine, *Le monde des femmes* (Paris: Fayard, 2005).

23 Vincent Descombes, *Le complément de sujet: Enquête sur le fait d'agir de soi-même* (Paris: Gallimard), 2004, p. 8.

24 Alain Renaut, *L'ère de l'individu* (Paris: Gallimard, 1989), p. 53.

25 Jean Bergeret, *Freud, la violence et la dépression* (Paris: Presses Universitaires de France, 1995).

26 Hans Joas, *The Creativity of Action* (Cambridge: Polity Press, 1996 [1992]).

27 Max Weber, *The Protestant Ethic and the Spirit of Capitalism* (New York: Dover, 2003 [1920]), p. 222.

28 Alain Touraine and Farhad Khosrokhavar, *La recherche de soi: Dialogue sur le Sujet* (Paris: Fayard, 2000), p. 149.

29 Danilo Martuccelli, *Forgé par l'épreuve* (Paris: Armand Colin, 2006).

30. Hans Joas, *G.H. Mead: A Contemporary Re-examination of His Thought* (Cambridge, Mass.: MIT Press, 1997 [1980]), p. 47.

31 Descombes, *Le complément de sujet*, p. 21.

32 Ibid., p. 263.

33 Cornelius Castoriadis, *World in Fragments: Writings on Politics, Society, Psychoanalysis, and the Imagination* (Stanford: Stanford University Press, 1997), pp. 165 and 167.

34 Cf., for example, Michel Foucault, *The Hermeneutics of the Subject: Lectures at the Collège de France, 1981–1982* (New York: Picador, 2005).

35 Louis Dumont, *Essays on Individualism: Modern Ideology in Anthropological Perspective* (Chicago: University of Chicago Press, 1991 [1983]).

36 Michel Wieviorka, *Violence: A New Approach* (London: Sage, 2009 [2005]), and more precisely the third part, which is entirely devoted to this question.

37 Touraine and Khosrokhavar, *La recherche de soi*, p. 135.

38 Ibid., p. 98.

39 Ibid., p. 188.

40 Maurice Godelier, *Au fondement des sociétés humaines: Ce que nous apprend l'anthropologie* (Paris: Albin Michel, 2007).

41 Touraine and Khosrokhavar, *La recherche de soi*, p. 155.

42 Primo Levi, *The Drowned and the Saved* (London: Abacus, 1989 [1986]).

43 Fernand Braudel, *Civilization and Capitalism, 15th–18th Centuries*, 3 vols (Berkeley: University of California Press,

1992 [1967–79]); Immanuel Wallerstein, *The Modern World-System, Vol. II: Mercantilism and the Consolidation of the European World-Economy, 1600–1750* (New York: Academic Press, 1980).

44 Thus the new entrepreneurs in post-Communist Russia, in the mid-1990s, sometimes claimed to be followers of the experience in Chile with an authoritarian political regime and a liberal economic one. Alexis Berelowitch and Michel Wieviorka, *Les Russes d'en bas* (Paris: Seuil, 1996).

45 Daniel Yergin and Joseph Stanislaw, *The Commanding Heights* (London: Simon and Schuster, 1997).

46 Signed on 22 July 1944, the Bretton Woods Agreements fixed the main lines of the working of the post-war international monetary and financial system.

47 By this expression, which was highly successful, particularly amongst the radical left, John Williamson designated the set of doctrines on which, according to him, the American Congress, the IMF, the World Bank, and various think-tanks had agreed to reform the economies of countries in crisis or in difficulty: control of budgets, liberalization of financial and trading markets, privatizations, deregulation, and so on.

48 Robert Reich, *The Work of Nations: Preparing Ourselves for 21st Century Capitalism* (New York: A.A. Knopf, 1991).

49 Viviane Forrester, *L'horreur économique* (Paris: Fayard, 1996).

50 Paul Michael Kennedy, *Preparing for the Twenty-First Century* (New York: Random House, 1993).

51 James Rosenau, *Turbulence in World Politics* (Princeton, NJ: Princeton University Press, 1990).

52 From the name of the Treaty of Westphalia, 1648, which set up the sovereign nation-state as the foundation of international law.

53 The article 'The Clash of Civilizations?' was published in the journal *Foreign Affairs*, 72(3), 1993, 22–49; the book was titled *The Clash of Civilizations and the Remaking of World Order* (New York: Simon and Schuster, 1996).

54 Nilüfer Göle, *Interpénétration: L'Islam et l'Europe* (Paris: Galaade, 2005).

55 David Harvey, *The Condition of Postmodernity: An Enquiry into the Origins of Cultural Change* (Cambridge, Mass.: Blackwell, 1990), p. 240.

56 Manuel Castells, *The Information Age: Economy, Society and Culture, Vol. III: End of Millennium* (Cambridge, Mass. and Oxford: Blackwell, 1998; second edition, 2000).

57 Quoted by Arjun Appadurai, *Modernity at Large: Cultural Dimensions of Globalization* (Public Worlds, Vol. 1) (Minneapolis: University of Minnesota Press, 1996), p. 77.

58 Ibid., p. 82.

59 This idea is found in particular in Mike Featherstone, Scott Lash, and Roland Robertson, *Global Modernities* (London: Sage, 1995).

60 Marc Abélès, Preface to Arjun Appadurai, *Après le colonialisme: Les conséquences culturelles de la globalisation* (Paris: Payot, 2001 [1996]), p. 11. (French translation of *Modernity at Large*.)

61 Ibid., p. 11.

62 Benedict Anderson, *Imagined Communities: Reflections on the Origin and Spread of Nationalism* (London: Verso, 1983).

63 Daniel Cohen, *Globalization and Its Enemies* (Cambridge, Mass.: MIT Press, 2006 [2004]).

64 Ibid., p. 143.

65 Ibid., p. 77.

66 Ibid., p. 166; Cohen, *La mondialisation et ses ennemis* (Paris: Grasset, 2004), p. 256. [The second part of the quotation is not included in the English edition – Trans.]

67 Michel Péraldi, 'Des *pateras* au transnationalisme: Formes sociales et image politique des mouvements migratoires dans le Maroc contemporain', *Hommes et Migrations*, June 2007. The *pateras* are the boats on which clandestine migrants attempt to reach Europe from Morocco.

68 Take for example the two exhibitions organized on this theme by Yvon Le Bot, in 2002 in the Parc de La Villette, 'Indiens: Chiapas-Mexico-Californie' (catalogue-book, Montpellier: Indigène éditions, 2002), and in 2006, 'Todos somos migrantes', Museo de la Ciudad, Mexico, 2006.

69 Cf. in particular Alejandro Portes, *Globalization from Below: The Rise of Transnational Communities* (Princeton, NJ: Princeton University Press, 1997), pp. 1–25; and Alain Tarrius, *La mondialisation par le bas* (Paris: Balland, 2002).

70 Cf. in particular Philip Mayer, 'Migrancy and the Study of African Towns', *American Anthropologist*, 64(3), 1962, 576–92: 'Migrancy commonly flows back and forth across

boundaries', and the best way to study it might be 'to begin at the study of the migrant persons themselves, by mapping out their networks of relations from the personal or egocentric point of view, as well as noting their part in the various structural systems' (p. 577), quoted by Nicholas De Maria Harney and Loretta Baldassar, 'Tracking Transnationalism: Migrancy and Its Futures', *Journal of Ethnic and Migration Studies*, 32(2), March 2007, 191.

71 Appadurai, *Modernity at Large*, pp. 37–8.

72 Ibid., p. 49.

73 Nina Glick-Schiller, Linda Basch, and Cristina Szanton-Blanc, *Towards a Transnational Perspective on Migration: Race, Class, Ethnicity, and Nationalism Reconsidered* (New York: New York Academy of Sciences, 1992).

74 Christine Inglis, 'Transnationalism in an Uncertain Environment: Relationship between Migration, Policy and Theory', *IJMS: International Journal on Multicultural Societies*, 9(2), 2007, 197–8 (*www.unesco.org/shs/ijms/vol9/issue2/art4*, accessed 23 September 2011).

75 Roger Waldinger and David Fitzgerald, 'Transnationalism in Question', *American Journal of Sociology*, 109(5), March 2004, 1177–95.

76 To use the expression coined by Ann M. Florini, *The Rise of Transnational Civil Society* (Washington, DC: Carnegie Endowment for International Peace, 2000).

77 James Beckford, 'Perspectives sociologiques sur les relations entre modernité et globalisation religieuse', in Jean-Pierre Bastian, Françoise Champion, and Kathy Rousselet (eds), *La globalisation du religieux* (Paris: L'Harmattan, 2001), p. 274.

78 Jean-Pierre Bastian, Françoise Champion, and Kathy Rousselet, 'Introduction', in Bastian et al. (eds), *La globalisation du religieux*, p. 14.

79 Roberto Motta, 'Déterritorialisation, standardisation, diaspora et identités: À propos des religions afro-brésiliennes', in Bastian et al. (eds), *La globalisation du religieux*, p. 63.

80 Cf., for example, Joseph Stiglitz, *Globalization and its Discontents* (New York: W.W. Norton, 2002).

81 George Ritzer, *The McDonaldization of Society* (London: Pine Forge, 1993).

82 Elie Cohen, *L'ordre économique mondial: Essai sur les autorités de régulation* (Paris: Fayard, 2001).

83 Ibid., p. 10.
84 Ibid., p. 11.
85 Pascal Lamy, Steve Charnovitz, and Charles Wyplosz, *Mondialisation et préférences collectives: La réconciliation?* (Paris: En temps réel, 2005).
86 Bertrand Badie, 'Nouvelles approches des relations internationales et du fait religieux', in Bastian et al. (eds), *La globalisation du religieux*, p. 265.
87 Cf. Geoffrey Pleyers, *Sujet, expérience et expertise dans le mouvement altermondialiste*, doctoral thesis (Paris: École des Hautes Études en Sciences Sociales, 2007).
88 Cohen, *L'ordre économique mondial*, p. 21.
89 Cf. the series of books by Mireille Delmas-Marty, *Forces imaginantes du droit* (Paris: Éditions du Seuil): Vol. 1 on *Le relatif et l'universel*, Vol. 2 on *Le pluralisme ordonné*, and Vol. 3 on *La refondation des pouvoirs* (2007).
90 Seyla Benhabib, 'Crépuscule de la souveraineté ou émergence de normes cosmopolites?', in Michel Wieviorka with Aude Debarle and Jocelyne Ohana (eds), *Les sciences sociales en mutation* (Auxerre: Éditions Sciences Humaines, 2007), p. 183.
91 Cf. Fuyuki Kurasawa, *The Work of Global Justice* (New York: Cambridge University Press, 2007).
92 Michel Foucher, *L'obsession des frontières* (Paris: Perrin, 2007).
93 Jean-François Bayart, *Le gouvernement du monde: Une critique politique de la globalisation* (Paris: Fayard, 2004), p. 18.
94 Ibid., p. 31.
95 John Ralston Saul, *The Collapse of Globalism: And the Reinvention of the World* (London: Atlantic Books, 2005).
96 Michel Aglietta and Laurent Berrebi, *Désordres dans le capitalisme mondial* (Paris: Odile Jacob, 2007), p. 7.
97 Ibid.
98 Ulrich Beck, *Cosmopolitan Vision* (Cambridge: Polity Press, 2006).
99 Saskia Sassen, 'L'émergence d'une multiplication d'assemblages de territoire, d'autorités et de droits', in Wieviorka et al. (eds), *Les sciences sociales en mutation*, p. 205.

Index